Boss

Bride

THE POWERFUL WOMAN'S PLAYBOOK FOR LOVE AND SUCCESS

Boss Bride

CHARREAH JACKSON

ST. MARTIN'S PRESS ♒ NEW YORK

BOSS BRIDE. Copyright © 2018 by Charreah Jackson. All rights reserved.
Printed in the United States of America. For information, address St. Martin's Press,
175 Fifth Avenue, New York, N.Y. 10010.

www.stmartins.com

Designed by Anna Gorovoy

The Library of Congress Cataloging-in-Publication Data is available upon request.

ISBN 978-1-250-12839-3 (hardcover)
ISBN 978-1-250-12841-6 (ebook)

Our books may be purchased in bulk for promotional, educational, or business
use. Please contact your local bookseller or the Macmillan Corporate and Premium
Sales Department at 1-800-221-7945, extension 5442, or by email at
MacmillanSpecialMarkets@macmillan.com.

First Edition: June 2018

10 9 8 7 6 5 4 3 2 1

To every woman who has ever wondered if all her dreams were possible and if she would have to choose between love and success. Boss Bride, you can have anything you can imagine and everything your heart desires. Expect the best from this big and crazy world.

To all the women who paved the way for us, starting with the shoulders I stand on: Cynthia Hutto Jackson, my mother, prayer warrior, confidence molder and inspiration; my grandmothers, Myrtha and Naomi, and their mothers, Cora and Katie.

To my daughter I have yet to meet, I am committed to making this world better for you and generations of women to come.

CONTENTS

INTRODUCTION

You were always destined to make a splash in this world, leaving every person, thing, and experience you encounter better than you found it. To use all your passion in pursuit of the very best life has to offer. You are a Powerhouse. This is your Playbook. This is your sacred space with the tools to breathe life into your latest personal and professional dreams. I know you are busy, so this book gets to the point. But before you up level your success and relationships, every good book should start with a good story. Here's mine:

As women around the country decided this is the year they would drop those stubborn ten pounds, I entered 2008 with the goal to gain at least two hundred pounds every two weeks. That's right. I wanted a full serving of a man across from me on a date at least twice a month. It didn't matter if he was tall, just my height in heels, rushing from his Wall Street job or coming from one of his gigs as a nonstarving artist, as long as he had a nice smile with solid values, lived with passion, and was steadily employed, I was open to meeting him.

I was two years into my life in New York City. I loved my job as a magazine editor and had settled into a spacious apartment where I watched *Sex and the City*'s Carrie Bradshaw and *Living Single*'s Regine Hunter. The two women showed off new shoes and new men regularly.

I had my sexy red stilettos. So where in the hell was my steamy love life?

I realized, like the job and the apartment, hot dates were not going to come find me. I had to be proactive in achieving the love life I craved. And let me tell you, my life transformed when I leaned into love.

Over the last ten years I've traveled the world learning the secrets of successful daters and couples, while navigating corporate America. I serve as a global speaker, dating and career coach, and the senior editor for Lifestyle & Relationships at *Essence* magazine. When "relationships" is in your job title, you get paid to hunt down the latest on love and be in everybody else's business. I've walked the streets of New York City asking women when they had their last orgasm and planned a surprise proposal for a couple who met through a story I worked on. I've interviewed more than one thousand people, including powerful women such as Hillary Clinton, Kerry Washington, and Sarah Jessica Parker. I've hosted focus groups, singles events, and dating workshops. I've gathered concrete evidence that NO, women don't have to choose between success and love, but we do have to be intentional to achieve both. What you are holding is your blueprint: how powerful women like you are unleashing their inner Boss Bride for personal and professional happiness.

So, what is a Boss Bride? She's a woman that fuses the characteristics of an effective boss—focused, strategic, delegator—with the best qualities of a bride at her wedding—happy, charming, living in the moment. Every woman can be a Boss Bride whether married ten years or unsure if she ever wants to head down the aisle. No matter your job title or relationship status, you can transform your life with the Boss Bride mentality and treat every day as your big day.

One of the reasons I wrote this book is because I started to feel women were succumbing to fears that the dreams for their personal lives weren't possible. That is crazy! There has been no other time in history that has been this good for ambitious women.

You have already defied data. You have already beaten the odds. Meeting your partner, having children (if you choose), and leading a life full of love is certainly within your reach. Alongside 500 million sperm, you outpaced them all and combined with a single egg, and here you are with a life and path unlike that of anyone else on the planet. You have the right to revel in the magic of your life. Do not be deterred by headlines. Stay focused on your goals and know you are more than enough to have everything you dream of.

The most important career decision you'll make is who you choose to marry.   —Sheryl Sandberg, COO of Facebook
                                    and author of *Lean In*

There is nothing passive about whom we love and how we live. Who sleeps in our beds and parents our children, and how we use our passion and power are the most important decisions we make. As Sheryl points out, our dating decisions and professional dreams directly impact one another.

We are a generation of women with the most professional opportunities and accomplishments of any women before us—which can be just as overwhelming as it is exciting. This book is a bridge to create a love life and career that fulfill you: it's time to Go HARD *and* go home.

When I asked women how their career and love lives influenced one another, they kept it real. Here's what a few had to say.

Each day I grow more optimistic about my career and more pessimistic about my love life. I fear I won't find a man who can understand, appreciate, and complement my hustle.
                              —Valerie, Los Angeles television producer

"My boss told me to take my wedding ring off once so I would be more desirable to a client."   —Tamara, New York business consultant

"I've seen a lot of women focus way more on work, and then wonder where their dating years have gone. After being advised by these women, I've decided to pay a bit more attention to my dating life and pursue a long-term relationship sooner than later."

—Berkeley graduate student

"As I continue to progress in my career, will my fiancé feel a certain way if he is not progressing on the same track?"

—L. Alexander, New York PR executive

"In my professional life, I am the expert and go-to woman that can get us to where we need to be. In my relationship, I want to be the 'you choose, dear' type of woman. I want to surrender the leadership role."

—Sharon, 38, nonprofit director

"First dates definitely ask about career goals. I've had guys also pry into my reasoning behind career decisions and ask about school loans. Recently a guy asked about my interest rates."

—Kirsten, 29, DC graduate student

As women continue to outnumber men on college campuses and open our own businesses at increasing rates, we are facing a new reality, which requires a modern approach to relationships. To crack the code on how powerful women maintain marriages and careers that curl their toes, I interviewed more than a hundred Working Wives to get their secrets along with tips from legendary Boss Brides such as First Lady Michelle Obama and Melissa McCarthy. You are holding insight from more than one thousand years of marriage and career success by accomplished women.

What This Book Breaks Down

- The Boss Bride Bill of Rights: 8 Permission Slips for Me, a Modern Woman
- Why your husband is the biggest decision of your career
- How powerful women manage work and family
- How to date like a pro—and meet men worthy of you
- The 6 most common dating personalities
- Why an engagement ring can rock your career
- Protect your fertility and plan your pregnancy
- How to Go HARD *and* go home
- 6 steps to finance your romance (YES, you should have a prenup)
- The Female Breadwinners' Survival Guide
- How to restart your life or relationships at any moment

No matter where you are in your love life or professional pursuits, there is a message for you in this book. If you've already settled into a great relationship (and YAY for love), I still encourage you to read it all. We need as many powerful women as possible to be informed and having discussions with other women on what's working in their relationships and careers. Each chapter includes insights from the Working Wives and closes with what each woman would whisper to herself while walking down the aisle at her wedding.

"You need to be loyal to your husband. You don't need to be loyal to your job. Unlike your husband, your job doesn't take a vow to be loyal to you. If you lose your job, your husband should be by your side. If you lose your husband, the only thing your job wants to know is how it will impact your work."

This is what one of our Working Wives would whisper. It is the reminder that we are much more than our job titles. The sad truth is many of us have poured more into our professional lives than into our personal happiness. We update résumés and LinkedIn pages but not our bucket lists and personal dream boards. It's your time to go full out for what your heart desires.

This is not a leisure read. This is an actual playbook with actions for you to take to get the life you desire. When it comes to the crucial decision of our joy and who we will share our love with, it's time to get off the sidelines to create the experiences we crave. Don't let men, money, or fear run your life. You hold the keys to your happiness.

Inside each chapter you will find the following:

- **The Ring:** As a Boss Bride your most important possession is a ring. Not a piece of jewelry but the ringing of your phone. Who picks up when you call? Who calls you? The quality of our lives is directly tied to the quality of our relationships. Each chapter includes The Ring, a prompt to pick up the phone and reach out to people in your life. Make those calls.

- **Save the Date:** To have what you've never had you will have to do what you've never done. The Save the Date is an assignment of specific steps toward adding more satisfaction to your life.

- **#BossBride Vow:** Dearly beloved, we've gathered to celebrate the greatness of you! Read these vows aloud as you commit to love on yourself through actions.

I took my "at least two dates a month" resolution seriously and have the stories to show for it all detailed in Chapter 3, Date Like a Pro (don't judge me). A year after setting my goal, I reconnected with a friend of a friend I first met at a Fourth of July party during my intern days in New York. That led to a first date at a Broadway show followed by a seven-year relationship where we were talking marriage. We'd discussed wedding locations and kids and I realized I didn't know everything I wanted to about being a wife who continued to pursue her passions. I had already made plenty of mistakes navigating my personal and professional passions, like that awkward argument on a work trip in Miami where I angrily whispered with my boyfriend in the hotel lobby hoping my client wasn't close by. I wanted to gather resources for myself and millions of other modern women on not having to choose between love and success. So I pitched this book you are now holding.

In a TV plot twist, the day I received the contract for my first book (hell yeah!), I left that long-term relationship (hell). It was time to move forward.

It was the ultimate #BossBride move: to do what felt right, even if it didn't make sense from the outside. And the timing was the worst; I had signed up to write a book with the word "bride" in the title while getting over a breakup. The good news was I always knew every woman could be a Boss Bride, no matter her job title or relationship status. I trusted everything would work itself out and my creator had me covered.

When you are bold enough to follow your heart, prepare for your dreams to be better than you imagined. A few months after my breakup, I met someone unexpectedly. He represented everything I needed (I had gotten clear on my checklist, which we will talk about in Chapter 3). I met him because I was first courageous enough to meet the best version of me and do what made her happy. He reflected back to me the love I had shown myself.

You have the opportunity to have everything your heart desires. To unleash a higher level of love and success in your life in the next month, I created a free Happily Ever Now playbook for you to get the most out of this book. Claim yours at www.bossbride.com/playbook.

Your power is contagious. By purchasing this book you have just invested in the future of another woman. Ten percent of the author's proceeds are donated to Dress for Success, the world's largest organization helping women return to the workforce and where I serve as a career coach.

Welcome aboard, Boss Bride.

The world is yours,
Charreah

1

YES, YOU ARE
A BOSS BRIDE

My great hope is to laugh as much as I cry, to get my work done and
try to love somebody and have the courage to accept the love in return.
—DR. MAYA ANGELOU

So let's get this straight: You are a Boss Bride.

I don't care what your job title or relationship status is. It doesn't matter if you have sworn off marriage or have never managed anyone in your entire life. It makes no difference if you are still finding your footing or recently retired. If you picked up this book and made it to this page, your spirit has acknowledged you want the best out of every area of your life and are ready to embrace your inner Boss Bride.

"And what exactly is a Boss Bride?" your side eye asks. She's a woman that fuses the characteristics of an effective boss—focused, strategic, delegator—with the best qualities of a bride at her wedding—happy, charming, and living in the moment.

Whether you've been working it for years or are unsure of your next step, you can adopt the Boss Bride mentality to achieve harmony in a hectic life, to be unbound while pursing your fullest potential with passion. Being a Boss Bride is stepping past your relationship status and job title to become the star of your own life. It is to treat every day like the best day of your life.

"Charreah, you have cancer," my doctor said two days after Christmas. I was nineteen and devastated. My parents drove me back to DC to pack up my dorm at Howard University and return home to Atlanta for six months of chemo followed by a summer of radiation. As I adjusted to this unexpected curveball, I was determined to not let a diagnosis crush my dreams. On my last day of radiation I walked out of the hospital to a packed van: my parents and I drove back to school that very same August day. I was the new managing editor for *The Hilltop*, my college newspaper founded by Zora Neale Hurston, and I had a job to do. I jumped back into school and took extra classes to graduate on time—and was grateful I did with Oprah Winfrey as our graduation speaker. Four days after her speech I moved to New York and my cubicle after flipping my summer internship into a job as an editorial assistant then magazine editor, my dream job. I was paying my rent by interviewing celebrities and sexy men.

"Your position is being eliminated," I was told in the height of the recent recession. That was about a year after learning I was the other woman in a new relationship, thanks to Google.

This is when I first became a powerful woman. To own that my happiness is always up to me and what looks like a failure can be an opportunity to grow. My setbacks taught me early to define and decide what my life would be. Now each sunrise, I tell today that it will be a good day, instead of letting the day decide my fate.

This is your opportunity to take a step back in your busy life to get clear that yes, your desires are yours for the taking. You came into this world with a mission to be your very best self and to enjoy enriching relationships that make it all worth it. It's time to get in the game and go for what you want!

I adopted the Boss Bride mentality and now wake up to a life I love. I have a powerful connection with my creator, get paid to make the world better, magnetize incredible opportunities (for example, I'm currently editing this chapter on a plane from South Africa), and have a community of friends, family, and soul mates who keep me smiling.

The first step in owning your rightful place in the world is to own that YES you are a Boss Bride. With that come inalienable rights to enforce. Read the following out loud.

Boss Bride Bill of Rights
8 Permission Slips for Me, a Modern Woman

1. I have the right to define joy and success for myself and actively seek them. I am responsible for my own happiness. I can live and love on my terms and can change my mind at any time.

2. I have the right to prioritize my personal life without sacrificing success. Who I spend my personal time with is just as important as my career. I can go hard *AND* go home.

3. I have the right to put caring for myself at the top of my to-do list every day. The better I take care of me, the more I have to give to the world.

4. I have the right to demand my worth in every scenario. I am worthy of respect at all times, the pay my talents merit, the relationships my heart craves, and anything else my soul desires.

5. I have the right to be vulnerable, which is a strength, not a weakness. My truth is my power.

6. I have the right to create boundaries in every area of my life and to teach people how to treat me.

7. I have the right to ask for help whenever I need it. Life is a team sport and I will actively seek support and community.

8. I have the right to live in the moment. This very second is one I will never see again so I will soak it all in.

Getting clear on your own power is essential in creating and maintaining a life you love. Every day we are teaching the world how to treat us by how we treat ourselves. Let your rights guide you as you commit to creating a life you love every day. And be honest, did you follow the instruction to read them out loud? That wasn't just to make you feel weird, but an opportunity for your entire body and the world around you to be reminded of your rights. Put the universe on notice on how you are to be treated. And get used to speaking up! The world needs your voice more than ever.

As Boss Brides we get to write our stories and make our own rules. Inside our Boss Bride Tribe Facebook group at bossbridetribe.com, women get real as we each carve out our own version of happy, and remind each other we always have options.

Identify the key people in your personal and professional life. Fill in the blanks:

_____ is my boss.

_____ is the love of my life.

Finished? Well, if either of those answers were not you go back and scratch through the name listed and put yourself.

YOU are your own boss. You may have managers and clients, but you are the ultimate decider of what industry you are in, how you make money, and how (and if) you work.

YOU are the love of your life. You are the only person you entered this world with and will spend every day with until you transition. You may have beautiful connections with others and a sexy soul mate to share your life with, but you will always be your first love.

The first and most essential step in changing your life is to realize it is up to YOU. Don't like something? Change it. Take control of your role as the CEO and love of your life.

Now that we've confirmed you are a Boss Bride, it's time we acknowledge something else: You are a powerhouse.

You are an unprecedented force unlike anything the world has ever seen. There never was anyone on this planet with your unique experiences, skills, and talents and there never will be again. You came to the world with a purpose and vision only you can fulfill. Every Wednesday in the Boss Bride Tribe we have Winsday, where we acknowledge what we've accomplished. In my coaching sessions with clients we explore what they have already accomplished before we jump into what they want to achieve. We often have a to-do list and need to add an it's done list to our routine. In your workbook (get your complimentary copy at www.bossbride.com), please take a moment and complete the My It's Done List and celebrate your incredible accomplishments so far. This is not a résumé recap but a real look at what you've achieved. Reflect on how powerful and badass you are. I've had clients who have bought multiple houses before the age of thirty, run marathons around the world, started businesses, published books, and saved lives. So why is finding a suitable partner and building a family so out of reach? Think about many of the things you have accomplished.

Some of our proudest moments are how we respond when adversity strikes. It's not the awards on my bookshelf that come to mind when I think of what I'm most proud. It's rebounding after losing my job, battling cancer, walking away from a relationship, risking falling in love again, and moving to a big city to chase my dreams. I was a bold badass with heart. And so are you.

How are you feeling? Seriously. In this moment. How do you feel? To be in tune with your feelings gives you access to true power. People who FEEL powerful create joy and transform the world. And people who don't FEEL powerful look past the power they have and spend their time trying to grab power. My It's Done List reminds me of my power in moments of self-doubt.

You Are Contagious

We all know someone who kills the mood whenever they join the party or that friend everyone hopes comes to brunch because it's always a good time when she's there (that's me—hey, gotta believe in yourself before anyone else does). The truth is every room you are ever in is impacted by your presence. Some people make us happy when they enter. Some people make us happy when they leave. Being a Boss Bride means being mindful of the impact you have in every scenario and every relationship. If something is missing, you have the opportunity to bring it into the room. Want more camaraderie at work? Take charge on connection. Wish your new boo took you on more dates? State your desires and make a Google doc of your dream dates for the season and hit that share button.

Once you get clear of just how amazing you are, you are in a position to better see ANYTHING is possible. We live in an abundant universe. Everything we enjoy was all once just an idea. The best thing you do for your future is to breathe into your biggest dreams.

What Do You Desire?

Write down your dreams for your life and explore the following prompts in your playbook.

- What I want to achieve
- Where and how I want to live

- Relationships I want
- Places I want to visit
- Experiences I want to have (e.g., skydiving, performing, teaching, making jewelry)
- Items I want to own

It is critical that you dream in detail and declare your biggest desires out into the world. Your vision for your life is your anchor and your guide. Each year I make a list of goals for that year to get me closer to my big dreams. I also make a twelve-month calendar grid listing all my tasks and big goals for the year. It helps me to not become overwhelmed and to have a big picture of my commitments so I don't overextend myself. For 2017 I added a TBD box and listed "Meet Oprah." The summer before I'd had the chance to meet the mogul herself, Dr. Oprah Winfrey, at an Essence Festival cocktail reception for the series *Queen Sugar*. Because I had never acknowledged I wanted to meet Oprah, it did not occur to me to make sure I met one of my biggest inspirations. When I got home and looked at the picture of Oprah on my wall, I realized I'd missed my shot. Originally in this book the next line read: *I won't make that mistake again and by the time you are reading this I will have made the connection happen.* Well, on April 18, 2017, my clear intention was supported by the universe and I met our Auntie Oprah. It was at the after party for the HBO film *The Immortal Life of Henrietta Lacks*, which she stars in. She came out of a corner I happened to be near. I walked right up and introduced myself. And she one-upped me by holding my face and saying "You are luminous." I don't remember what she said after that, because Oprah. I debated not washing my face ever again. It happened because I got crystal clear that I wanted to meet her and actively pursued opportunities for that to happen—and the universe handled the rest.

In addition to my big goals, I have a life plan of where I hope to be in the next few years. Having a life plan helps me integrate my personal and professional goals. I probably won't go on a busy book tour the same year I hope to have a baby. And knowing I want to have a baby helps me have important conversations with my doctors (which we will get to later in this book).

Stretch for Your Dreams

To have what you've never had you will have to be willing to do what you've never done. To fully embrace being a Boss Bride you will have to leave the confines of your comfort zone. Your dreams will require you to stretch. It was uncomfortable waiting to introduce myself to Oprah Winfrey and absolutely worth it. Right now fling your arms out and stretch your limbs. Move your neck around. Feel the muscles in your body move.

That's what happens when we stretch in our actions and thoughts. We work out the kinks and build our muscles. My biggest inspiration for stretching is my favorite animal: the giraffe. What I love about giraffes is their regal appearance and ability to rise above it all, which wasn't always the case. The tallest animal wasn't always tall with a long neck. In fact, one of the giraffe's closest relatives is the okapi, a short horselike animal with zebra-striped legs that stands around five feet tall.

So how did giraffes get to be so much taller than their shorty cousins? By stretching beyond their comfort zone. While in Orlando World for the Disney Dreamers Academy, where I've taught journalism for the last few years, I got a chance to visit Disney's Animal Kingdom. I learned there that giraffes grew longer necks over time in response to heavy competition for food in the savanna. Being hungry pushed them to evolve and grow taller to reach food. The okapi didn't face much competition in the rainforest and didn't grow over time. It was adversity and a willingness to persevere that grew giraffes over time. Like a boss.

To have new opportunities and experiences, you will have to stretch new muscles.

YOUR STRETCHING CHEAT SHEET

STEP 1: TAKE STEADY STEPS

Giraffes did not grow five feet in five months. Decide what first step you can take to expand beyond your usual behaviors, such as smiling back at the barista who always tries to flirt or telling a few friends you will let them be the first to read the new novel you are writing.

STEP 2: LET GO OF LOOKING GOOD

"The stretch is the distance between your comfort zone and your dream," says my friendtor and Boss Bride Teneshia Jackson Warner. She learned stretching firsthand after quitting her job and moving across the country to chase her dream of a career that made a difference. We won't always look the cutest to others while letting go of the familiar. Teneshia left a "good" corporate position to pursue her bigger dream of mixing social good and entertainment. Many who loved her thought she had lost her mind. "I moved to New York with no job, two bags, a Bible, and *The Prayer of Jabez*," she says. "I was okay to look crazy to follow my dream."

STEP 3: TRUST YOURSELF

There is usually a gap between what we are called to do and what we feel we are capable of doing. In order to fill the gap you must trust and take leaps of faith. "I have not met a dreamer to date whose vision was able to be accomplished in their comfort zone," Teneshia adds. In moments of doubt, remind yourself that you are an infinite woman with unlimited power.

> This book will ask you to do things outside of your comfort zone. Anytime something feels uncomfortable interrogate what about it makes you uncomfortable. And ask yourself: **What is my comfort costing me?**

Ask for What You Want

I bonded with one of my favorite Boss Brides Niecy Nash at a sex toy shop a few years ago. We traveled around Los Angeles for a video series in partnership with the *Fifty Shades of Grey* film, exploring ways women can tap into their sexy—from role-playing to getting a few pleasure products. And that day happened all because Niecy was willing to stretch. Fifteen years ago the Emmy-winning actress was answering phones for an airline. After marrying in her early twenties, Nash then welcomed three young children to their family. But the young mom knew there was an entertainer in her busting to get out and be on TV. She went to her husband with a request.

"Can you give me nine months to make it work for this dream? I've given my body over three times to another human being for nine months. Can I have your support for nine months for me? If I can't make it work, I'll go back to work full-time and we won't have this discussion again," she said. He agreed to hold things down as she gave her dream one final push. Over those months Niecy went to auditions all over Los Angeles, sometimes taking her young children with her and turning the lobby into an impromptu daycare when a last-minute callback happened. As she neared the end of her nine months she still hadn't landed any work. Then within two weeks she booked her role as host of *Clean House*, which went on to win an Emmy, and a starring role on the Comedy Central show *Reno 911*. "I was right to bet on myself," Niecy said, many roles later, as we ate breakfast in New York's Meatpacking District. "God doesn't put a dream in you not to use it." I was interviewing the star for her first cover of *Essence* to promote her new TNT series *Claws*, which has become a bona fide must-see.

Stretching beyond our comfort zone is where the magic lives. And one of life's biggest stretches is to allow ourselves to be vulnerable enough to experience the magic of love.

As I shared in the introduction, the same day I received the contract to write this book, I walked away from a long relationship that had been heading to marriage. It was my biggest Boss Bride move yet: to do what was best for me and not focus on how it could look or impact others. We didn't break up over one major infraction. Over our time together I'd continued to grow and so did my needs. I evolved to look at myself and life differently. I could see the cracks in our relationship that I had been avoiding; the slowing of our communication and un-aired grievances. I realized our relationship had run its course. It was my own self-fulfilling prophecy. Two years before I had walked into 30 Rock to be a guest on *The Meredith Vieira Show* alongside the cofounder of Tinder Sean Rad and sexologist and TV host Logan Levkoff, PhD, to talk dating. A woman in the crowd asked when do you know it's time to move on. I quipped, "If you are asking that question it may be time to move on." Well, I was right. It was time I moved forward. I trusted that everything was still happening the way it was supposed to, though it wasn't all easy. It was a process to let go of what I thought was my future. I spent the summer falling in love with myself and giving my heart permission to dream again.

A few months after my breakup I met a guy. More like my spirit collided with this magnetic soul housed in a six-foot-two dark frame. My roomie Kelly and I went for dinner at 67 Orange Street, a sultry bar in Harlem around the corner from our duplex. We danced in our seats as this tall man danced on the floor. Then he danced his way to our table. After the song cut off, he started to walk away. I stood on the bar-stool rung and yelled to him, "Really?" My southern sensibility was offended he would shimmy and not say hello. He came back and introduced himself.

We'll call him Sir Brooklyn. He was a brilliant and caring writer and musical artist from Brooklyn who has had music videos on MTV. Now he taught writing at a charter school in Harlem while continuing to create music. He and some of his coworkers had come to 67 Orange, a few blocks from their school. I was fresh out of a breakup so I was not remotely thinking about dating because I was still hoping things might work out with my former partner. Sir Brooklyn and his friends invited us to a bar in Brooklyn. The night felt magical and we went from Harlem to Brooklyn, which is basically LA to Atlanta in NY distance. On the train ride over it dawned that there may be some interest from Sir Brooklyn. Somehow the others walked ahead of us once we got to Brooklyn and he and I made our way to the bar, where we fell into a deep conversation. And I told him my situation of recently leaving a long relationship. He replied, "I believe in love. You should fight for that." I was surprised and appreciative he didn't sidestep where I was emotionally. He then added: "And if that doesn't work out, I'd like to take you out on a date." We all danced. And smiled in the photo booth before Kelly and I headed back to Harlem.

A week later Sir Brooklyn and I talked on the phone for the first time and have talked hours on end ever since. I became the cliché of "when you aren't looking." The truth is more nuanced. Coming out of a relationship gave me a fresh start to fall in love with myself at a higher level. To recommit to me. And that is a potent magnet for someone with substance. Sir Brooklyn introduced me to Chani Nicholas, a brilliant astrologer with a degree in feminist counseling. Each week she shares horoscopes at chaninicholas.com. They are profound and life affirming. As a new moon entered my sign of Aquarius a few days before my birthday and the deadline for this book, her words hit home. She spoke to the reality of any woman going full out for her dreams and all that comes with stepping into your new season.

AFFIRMATIONS BY CHANI NICHOLAS

I use Friday's new moon to renew my relationship to myself. My life is not a popularity contest. I live my life in a way that makes me feel right with myself. Being liked isn't the point.

Being able to like myself, however, is. I will regenerate myself. My energy comes from within and I honor what I need to do in order to refuel. The whole world might need me, but when I am in need I make sure I am filled up first. With a renewed energy, with a packed schedule, with the phone possibly ringing off the hook, I balance the intensity of my days with the self-care that I crave. The increase of activity I experience now is not an accident. All things that come through my door have been awaiting my arrival as well. I am ready for the onslaught of responsibility and in that I stay accountable to myself and to my health.

Being a Boss Bride is to always love ourselves first, to fill our cups, and share the overflow with others. For too long I gave my portion for myself away and wondered why I was so depleted. After reading Chani's affirmation, I followed up on doctors' appointments and confirmed all my new insurance accounts. The more we love on us, the more we have to give.

I first met my coworker Mary at a New Year vision board party I hosted for the company. It was Mary's first time making a vision board and she put engagement rings all over her board. I saw her again a few months later and this time she was with her fiancé and couldn't wait to tell me how he never saw the board but got the ring she wanted. Less than two years later they were married.

The truth is nothing is magic. Gemstones, vision boards, affirmations, and goal lists aren't genies to give you what you want. But people who actively are responsible for their energy, get clear on their desires, and declare into the universe what they actually want make it much easier for good things to find them. When you are clear on your desires you are also more likely to take actions in alignment with your dreams. My life changed when I got courageous enough to say what my heart truly desired in detail.

What keeps many of us from saying out loud what we want for our future is our past. Before I leaned into my desires I was cheating on my dreams with my past pain. By the time you've made it to reading this book, life has served you some highs and lows. Some laughter and pain. Old wounds and disappointment can have us doubtful if our dreams are within our reach.

Embrace Your Journey

In order to have the life you dream of you have to be honest about where you've come from. Over six months, I worked on myself like never before through personal development training with Momentum Education. And one chance encounter had me in a depressive funk for two months.

It started with an innocent text from my old friend Justin: "Met your dad at work. Lol."

Justin lived back home in Atlanta and was working at the CDC like my dad. He and I had met in the fourth grade when we started in the magnet program together at Browns Mill Elementary in Decatur, Georgia. We were close classmates from then through college, stopping at Miller Grove Middle School and Southwest DeKalb High School along the way. We had gone to each other's birthday parties, taken trips together, and there was that unfortunate time I almost hit his mom with my mom's car shortly after I got my license. Our crew partied together and went to prom. He, my best friend Celeste, and I all went to Howard University, where we perfected our spades skills. I went to his gorgeous wedding in New Orleans and even featured him in *Essence*, where he talked about how his wife's flirting with him led to their relationship.

On this fateful fall day Justin and my dad happened to be sitting in a training session together. From growing up he remembered my dad's name was Jerry and he realized it was indeed the same guy.

I laughed as he told me the story of them meeting and him helping my dad with his computer in the training. The next day I cried.

How had I been friends with Justin since fourth grade and my dad never met him?

Oh yeah, that's right. Up until I was fourteen my dad lived across the country in California and I saw him once or twice a year during Christmas and summer. Since he returned to Georgia my dad and I built a close relationship. We watched shows together and he made sure my favorite foods were around when I came home. He loved me and showed it.

But I never fully acknowledged the pain of his absence in my child-hood and the memories that could never be re-created to include him. I was stunned at how skillfully I had hid that wound from my-self. And when I took the scab off the pain started to ooze out. I could see how something I never noticed or acknowledged had impacted my whole life.

I could see why in college I was so busy guarding my heart that I didn't realize I was the prize. It explained why I liked men but never expected much from them.

It explained my trust issues I discovered while doing training with Momentum.

Though I was naturally warm and friendly, it was not easy to actu-ally be my friend. I was a lone wolf. The first man who was supposed to love me had fallen down on the job and I learned early I should only expect to depend on myself.

A few weeks after my dad and Justin met I went to dinner with my mentor Sylvia High. I recounted to her my epiphany and the dormant pain I was swimming in. I cried into my meal and asked her, "How did I hide this from myself?" She replied, "You made up a story that had you be okay. Now that you are strong enough, you are facing it."

And face it I did. The person who had lied the most to me was me. That meant I could also start to tell myself the truth.

I cried for the first time for the baby that had been left because her daddy moved away when she was only one. It wasn't until I acknowledged the ways my parents' divorce and my father's leaving affected me that I could truly start to heal the scars of abandonment and distrust I didn't realize had been coloring every relationship I entered. When I sat in the pain I had been running from all my life, I could see how it had been keeping me from letting others get close.

What shifted my perspective on the pain was a conversation with my brother. He reminded me I wouldn't be the woman I am if anything in the past had been different. I wouldn't be writing to you and you would not have the blessings in your life if our lives had been different. That reality helped me start to release the anger. Once I began to let go of the pain, I found gratitude and grace. I was grateful my parents found each other and had my brother and me. I celebrated them for who they were—two descendants of South Carolinian slaves with fathers who didn't get the chance to complete high school and who both had master's degrees. They had leaped out of the rural South to create a life for themselves. But all of their education never included how to sustain a healthy relationship. They did the best they could and I was always loved.

It felt like a weight lifted off me that I didn't realize I was carrying. Being free from that fear and pain meant I could go toward my desires instead of running away from what I didn't want: to be hurt by a breakup. I could ask myself what I wanted instead of focusing on what I feared.

Releasing old pain gave me the courage to confront anything else in my life that wasn't completely aligned. I was in a seven-year relationship. I had to face the ways we both had transformed over that time frame. I had to acknowledge the young woman who guarded her heart fiercely with fear had grown up and her needs had changed.

We ended the relationship. It wasn't easy to walk away. But being out of a relationship meant I got to focus on myself and unpack everything that led me to the current moment. I went surfing for the first time and started trying more new things.

The Ring: Own Your Story

After grieving my parents' divorce thirty years after they split, I had honest conversations with both of them to understand their decision and them as people. It's your turn to cleanse your heart to create space for your new season. Call someone connected to your past. Fill in the blanks and make peace with your history.

Sometimes you've got to let everything go—purge yourself . . . If you are unhappy with anything . . . whatever is bringing you down, get rid of it. Because you'll find that when you're free, your true creativity, your true self comes out.   —Tina Turner

Make Room for Your New

Tina Turner knows all about letting go to create space for love. She got married at age seventy-three to her younger man who she had been with for twenty-seven years. She let go of old heartache and trauma to create space for love and the vulnerability it requires.

So often we walk through life with our fists closed, afraid we will lose what we have. Nothing can get out and nothing can get in. To have the life you crave you will have to be willing to open your hands and heart, and give up what you have to create space for even more.

Often while coaching women a shadow starts to appear in the room and in the conversation. She is still holding on to pain from the past or hope that some guy or boss will come around and start to treat her right. Residue from the past can taint your future and attract emotionally unavailable people. The first step to great love and success is to create space in your life and heart. Before you can invite someone new into your space, you have to clear out the ghosts of the past.

In my Happily Ever Now course we have an entire module on Releasing with Love. That means letting go of anything holding you down including old heartache, skirts with broken zippers, jobs that have expired, and anything else not actively supporting you.

What will you heal and release? Anything that's holding you back, we have to let go. Often the universe is waiting for us to make room for the things we desire. Hanging on to the memories and hurt feelings from the past can cloud your future. Before continuing the journey to find your next level, lighten up in six steps.

How to Pack Light

1. NAME YOUR PAIN
We cannot heal what we won't address. Before we can transform our hurts, we first have to take a serious look at what we've been through. You get to address every hurt. You get to say out loud what has sucked about life from getting sick to heartache and regret. When 30-something Simone explored the wreckage from her crushing breakup, she realized that while her ex was "good on paper," he was also arrogant and unsupportive when her mother became sick. Realizing he wasn't built for the long haul helped her better understand what she did want.

2. FIND FORGIVENESS
One of the most crucial components in preparing for your future is a gift from you to you: compassion. Let go of the anger over what hap-

pened. In addition to freeing yourself of any anger, you have to leave behind thoughts of *I should have known better* or *Why didn't I see this coming?* Even if a situation doesn't end as you would have liked, you can still make peace with the situation. Everything in your life is building you for better. Say it with me: I forgive them. I forgive me.

3. SIFT OUT THE GOOD

Everything we've been through led us to this very moment and is building us for better. After you acknowledge what you've been through comes the chance to release the bad and keep the lessons. Healing lets us let go of what didn't work. Any time forgiving and healing feels like too much work, lean on love for yourself and the life you desire. Love is our most powerful force.

4. BUILD YOUR BOUNDARIES

In healing, we get to forgive ourselves for any time we've put ourselves in harm's way and decide how people will treat us moving forward. Taking ownership of our bodies and our happiness means we get to let others know what does and does not work for us. One of the best pieces of advice I ever heard was from Susan L. Taylor ten years ago: *Not everyone deserves a front row seat in your life.* As you get clear on your needs, you will be discerning of who gets to be close to you. The beauty of abundance is there is room in the balcony. Let people earn their way to the front row, sometimes even people we love. It is dangerous to have the wrong people close to you.

5. GET OUT OF YOUR OWN WAY

A former partner or old pain aren't the only things that can block new love and opportunities. Sometimes the holdup is the gorgeous woman in the mirror and she's holding off on love out of choice. America now has the highest number of single-headed households in the nation's history. Not only are we marrying less often but also later in life, creating more time to settle into a "doing me" routine. After her first marriage ended, *Steve Harvey Morning Show* cohost

Shirley Strawberry got comfortable in her independent woman status and busy career, only to realize she hadn't seriously dated anyone in more than five years. "It felt liberating but there were also some lonely nights," she says. Strawberry made a conscious effort to attract love by mentally preparing to share her space and giving men who approached her more than a quick glance. She's now traded in weekends of shopping and *Law & Order* marathons for snuggling or cooking with her new husband. "When you make room for love, you discover you have more than enough space," she says.

6. SHARE YOUR STORY

"If you are silent about your pain, they'll kill you and say you enjoyed it," Zora Neale Hurston told us. Yet too often women, especially those of us who the world thinks have it together, hide our heartache. The sweetest part of healing is it frees you from the sting of your experience—and any judgment of others. As you heal, share your journey with others. Your testimony is needed, and may be your ticket to your next season.

Thankfully, our hearts are not like a closet. The more love you add, the more you have room for. Don't get bogged down in the notion of losing or finding the One. Enjoy each experience for what it is, whether he was "the one who taught you to change a tire" or "the one you'll tell your granddaughter about." Create space for love to wow you.

Save the Date: Lighten Up

In the next week, commit to release at least three items in your home that no longer serve you, and schedule a purge day in your calendar every month. Start with clothes that don't fit, you don't wear, or don't make you feel amazing; kitchen and bathroom products you don't use; and towels and lingerie that have seen their best days. The more you let go, the more you have room to receive. Also physically purge any reminders or digital connections to past partners.

I was walking to work one morning when a thought stunned me. I was thinking of the relationship I had left when I realized how I had been waiting for someone else to marry me and treasure me. I wanted someone else to make vows they would never hurt me when I had never vowed to never hurt me. I wanted someone else to think I was the most beautiful girl in the world, when I didn't always acknowledge my beauty in my own bedroom. I wanted someone to send me my favorite flower when I hadn't taken the time to know what my favorite flower was. I wanted to be pampered at my favorite spa when I didn't have a favorite spa.

People don't treat you how you treat them. People treat you how you treat yourself. When you love on yourself and enforce your boundaries, you teach others to do the same. I wanted someone to marry me when I hadn't been madly in love with my own self.

How could I vow to give my best to someone else when I hadn't given my best to myself? How could I expect my marriage to work with someone else when I wasn't all in with the relationship with myself?

I decided I would commit to giving my very best to me. As a celebrant and officiant, I've spoken at weddings and memorial services. By far my favorite ceremony was making vows to my own self. I looked in the mirror and promised to always be there for me, to be there for myself for better or worse, in sickness and health, as long as I lived. It was the best gift I gave myself—and my future spouse: to commit to fall deeper in love with myself every day.

I challenge you to make vows to yourself in the playbook. The more you love on you the more you create space for your dreams. At any moment you can say YES, *I will commit to give my best to me*. Remember YOU are the love of your life and she deserves your consistent care and compassion. You may now treasure the bride you are.

Dearly Beloved

Now that we've talked about the beauty of life and love, let's talk about death. YAY. Everyone's favorite topic. I know, I know. Way to keep things exciting. Well, whether we like it or not, death is a natural part of life. Around 2015, I went to about ten funerals in a little over a year. I come from big families on both sides and we had older relatives pass away including my grandmother Naomi, my last living grandparent. Celebrating their lives and grieving the losses reminded me how precious life is.

The beauty of living with intention is you don't have to wait until death calls to think about the legacy you want to leave. One of the best exercises I ever completed was to write my own eulogy. That's right, I imagined what my best friend would say at my funeral. She would share my impact on the world, how passionately I loved, and how I dropped it and brought it back up at my eightieth birthday party.

"Begin with the end in mind" is habit number two for Stephen Covey's 7 *Habits of Highly Effective People*. And for a Boss Bride that includes thinking about the end of our lives and how we want to spend the precious years we have on the planet. When I wrote my eulogy, I could see dreams for my life that I had not had the courage to say out loud, things I thought I would get to "later." All of a sudden I had run a large business and produced a TV series, something I hadn't admitted before that time. In my Happily Ever Now course students write their eulogies, which is reviewed as one of the favorite exercises. I encourage you to join us and get clear on the legacy you hope to leave and write your eulogy in your playbook. (Haven't grabbed yours? Download it at www.bossbride.com/playbook.)

Every eulogy includes other people. Relationships are the most important investment we make in this life and what last forever. Going to all those funerals made me keenly aware of how our bonds with others shape our experiences.

I was able to see each person's funeral front row: our inner circle that sends us off from this world. Think about who would be in the front row at your funeral and the people whose funeral you would be on the front row for. What are your relationships like with those people? When did you last spend time with each of them? Which relationships would you like to be stronger?

It's not our bosses or coworkers who tend to us in sickness and death, but our family and friends. Those in the front row deserve the best of us.

Your Love & Success Squad

Every big blessing in my life has come through the people in my life. I have met my best friends through other friends. Both times I was hired at *Essence* someone contacted me. I met Sir Brooklyn because my sister-friend Kelly was determined for us to go out on a Monday night. You are holding this book because my friend Adenike Olanrewaju connected me to my literary agent Regina Brooks. I met Oprah because my girl Alicia Quarles invited me out with her to an HBO event.

The quality of your life lives in the quality of your relationships. As a Boss Bride, it is essential that you identify and cultivate your support system to have the life you desire. People are the key to unlocking success and happiness. Assess your network for the following roles in your life.

My Team: The people who help bring my dreams to life. This includes consultants, lawyers, designers, coaches, assistants, and interns.

My Support: These are people who keep me feeling encouraged and care about me as a whole person, not just my success.

My Sponsors: The powerful people who vouch for me and are in a position to support me with big opportunities. They may not have a lot of time but come through when it counts.

My Advisers: The accomplished people who give sound insight and guidance. These are my mentors and guides.

My Protégés: The young people who can learn from me. I can touch the future by shaping a young person.

My Rabbits: The people who inspire me in this season and show me what's possible for my next. They are a few steps ahead of me and keenly remember being where I am now.

In your playbook, complete the Love & Success Squad chart to get clear on your support system. As you upgrade your life you will evolve and expand your circle. One of the things I love most about the Boss Bride Tribe is seeing likeminded women meet for the first time. Commit to pouring yourself into your network so when you need a net it works. One of the best pieces of advice I ever got was to cultivate relationships before you need them. You never know when you will need to make a call or request, so invest in people while you can so that you have a reserve to sip from.

Yes, You Are a Bride

For a lot of women in the Tribe who aren't married it's not the "Boss" that's uncomfortable to own, it's the "Bride." *But how am I a Boss Bride if I'm single or divorced?* Owning that you are a bride is about embodying the qualities of a woman on her wedding day—every day. To greet each morning like it is the best day of your life because it is the only day you have at this moment. Olympic gold medalists don't think of themselves as Olympic gold medalists for the first time when they are getting a medal. They often have spent more than a decade preparing to claim their prize often decided in less than twenty minutes of their life. To become an Olympian they had to envision themselves as an Olympian years before. Every great athlete shares the story of imagining their career long before it happened. So yes, you are a Bride and get to embody the state of mind of one! As I type to you, I know I am a wife without being engaged. Standing in my power as a wife guides me to make decisions that help me prepare for my future instead of doubting if my dreams are real. I write notes to my husband and encourage you to do the same in your playbook. Writing to my husband reminds me he is a real person already walking around the planet. I include him in my prayers and hope he is having a good day. There is power in our words and putting the world on notice of where we are headed.

If you are still having trouble with your innate right as a Boss Bride, where else are you uncomfortable fully stepping into your power? Is it at work? Is it with your family or friends? Is it with the new guy or your husband of three years?

Take Your Seat

After all we've covered, you still may be wondering if you are a Boss Bride. And if you are, that, my sister, may be your imposter syndrome kicking in.

In between my editor gigs at *Essence* I worked as the social media manager at a fashion and beauty PR firm for two years where I spearheaded social media strategy for brands like TRESemmé and covered fashion week in New York and Miami. And for the first year I had serious imposter syndrome, defined as high-achieving individuals who are marked by an inability to internalize their accomplishments and a persistent fear of being exposed as a fraud.

That was me waiting for someone to tap on my shoulder and be told this was all a mistake. And I wasn't alone in feeling fraudulent. Sheryl Sandberg, Emma Watson, Maya Angelou, and Kate Winslet have all admitted to imposter syndrome and feeling out of place with their success at some point. I have worked to build my worthy muscle. I am currently writing to you with my feet up in a business class seat to South Africa. I've had a few glasses of Méthode Cap Classique, South Africa's sparkling wine. Before I could get comfortable with the perks,

I had to get comfortable with being worthy of every good thing that comes my way. You are worthy of every opportunity that comes your way. There is nothing and no one out of your league.

Being a Boss Bride is grabbing your power in every area of your life. To take your seat at the table. The sooner we embrace what we desire, the sooner it will manifest in reality.

To be a Boss Bride is a privilege not afforded to every woman in the world yet. In some countries women can't vote or travel without a man. Up until the 1970s women in America couldn't have their own credit cards. To women who have the option to live freely, we owe it to those who don't to live out loud and help create a world where all women have the opportunity to reach their highest potential. When we raise our own vibration, we raise all women.

I was reminded of this at the United Nations' International Women's Entrepreneurship Day summit. Walking onto the global headquarters for peace and seeing all the flags and history of the world, I owned the fact that I belonged there and took my seat at the table while listening to speakers. I was especially smitten with speaker HRH Crown Princess Katherine of Serbia, philanthropist and patron of Lifeline Humanitarian Organization. She was petite and packed with wisdom like "Take control of yourself. Then you can control the rest of the world. Let your life speak." Beneath the royal title was a real woman who knew love is always our secret weapon. "I don't wear a crown. My heart is my crown and we can all have a crown there."

You are royalty. Think about everything that went right for you to be reading this book (thank you). When we check into how magical our lives are we are less concerned with what it looks like to others.

#BossBride Vow

- I will pursue my happiness with urgency.
- My happiness and goals are within reach.

Get clear on your rights, your dreams, and your Love & Success Squad with your personal playbook available at www.bossbride.com/playbook to put your thoughts in one place and track your progress.

In this life, sometimes we get to choose our own adventure. When it comes to relationships, it is especially important that we pick up the pen and craft our own romance. What will your story be?

Whispers of a Woman
WHAT EACH WORKING WIFE WOULD SAY TO HERSELF AS SHE WALKED DOWN THE AISLE

Life is going to happen to us but always remember why we fell in love and always invest in yourself. **The best is yet to come!** Live in your POWER at all times and in every moment. This doesn't mean my way is the only way. It means be confident in my own voice and open to all possibilities. I'm stronger than any challenge I will ever face. **Be true to YOU! Follow what you desire, don't be afraid to speak up, don't be afraid to walk away.** Cherish each moment. Find something positive to focus on. **Enjoy and be present.** Marriage is a lifetime commitment. You may fall in and out of love over the years but remember you must be as committed to this marriage as you are to breathing.

2

PRIORITIZE LOVE

The most important career decision you'll make is who you choose to marry.
—SHERYL SANDBERG

I had an orgasm in my heart.

Yes, you read that right. I have had an orgasm in my heart. Literally. The uncontrollable spasms and constriction of my muscles. The release. The euphoria.

And it took me by complete surprise. Until the moment it happened to me I didn't know it was possible. Now I know you can have an orgasm in any of your seven main chakras and beyond. Though we are socialized to focus on our sexual organs, you can experience overwhelming joy in any of your energy centers. I learned this and so much more at the Healing the Heartspace Retreat by Jason Hairston and Jay English, two energy healers and spiritual teachers. The weekend consisted of the powerful duo leading us in connecting with our own hearts and using the planet's most powerful force, love, to heal others and ourselves.

I was in the midst of Jason and Jay's signature twin power healing session using quantum energy healing when the heart orgasm happened. I was lying on a table with my eyes closed as the two men worked to release any trapped energy in my body. They bathed me in sound and sent positive energy into me as I felt my mind and spirit begin to travel. I felt myself inside my mother's womb at the hospital when I was born and felt her love as people visited. I talked to my former partner as he reminded me we hadn't failed but completed the roles we were to play in each other's lives. I saw me and the new guy Sir Brooklyn in the 1800s sitting on a porch. I heard my first Sunday school teacher and early Boss Bride inspiration Mrs. Mable Hall Clark singing "He's Got the Whole World in His Hands," her favorite song. We'd sung it at her funeral a few months prior. My hands involuntarily lifted from my sides as I felt old energy release out of my palms. And my heart contracted as love pulsed through my veins and I felt how loved I have been my whole life. I felt euphoric as my heart clenched. At our core, we are all simply love.

When Jason invited me to the event in November, I was nearing the end of the most emotional year of my life. I had been cleansing the thirty-year wound of my parents' split and my father moving away, and all the ways it had impacted me up until then. I also was a few months out of my breakup. That September I went to Sylvia High's I Am Woman Conference in Atlanta. At the previous conference it clicked with me that women are God's masterpiece. After creating the universe and everything in it—nature, waterfalls, rainforests, plants, animals— God created a man, and then the finale: a woman. At this year's conference Sylvia asked us a simple question: How is power different for men and women?

The ladies at my table began to discuss the varying ways women and men approach power. It dawned on me that women are so powerful as creators and caregivers that men are called to protect and provide for us. It's not because we are weak that we should be cared for, but because we are so valuable we deserve protection and provision. We are the planet's most loving creatures and the only being that can birth humanity. Of course that is sacred and deserves to have support. Of course strong powerful men should clear the way for Queens. I realized I didn't always expect to depend on other people, especially men. And it was time that changed. It wasn't about needing someone else but realizing I was worthy of being cared for on my journey.

It felt like the minute I opened up to love and anticipated support I could see men showing up for me. The guy that held the train door as I waltzed down the stairs or my Friday night yoga teacher sitting in front of the door during meditation to keep our time sacred from disruption. That included Jason inviting me to the Healing the Heartspace Retreat.

And there I was cleansing my heart chakra and being reminded there are great men in the world who want to support us.

Love is our most powerful emotion. Love is who we are at our core before pain and fear enter the picture.

Before my heart knew it could orgasm, we started that day exploring the definition of love. My definition of love had been when action and emotion meet in service and sacrifice to another. It's not enough to say the right things and not act on it. It's not enough to do the right things and have it not be from a genuine place of care. We all know someone who does things with an attitude: #NoThanks. For me love was the marriage of what we think, say, and do.

Jason and Jay's definition was that love is oneness in motion. Love is when two spirits are joined and move through life in sync. I liked the simplicity of that definition and how easy it is to see if it's love: if you are joined and operating as one. When you are one with another what impacts them impacts you. When we are one with another we are considerate and compassionate. To hurt them is to hurt ourselves (nod to Beyoncé). To tap into love is to allow another to truly sync inside our hearts. Love is having a shared vision. When we don't share the same vision that is division and division leads to divorce and separation. In any relationship where you want more love, it starts with uniting.

One of the essential elements to being a Boss Bride living with passion and peace is to prioritize love. To know we deserve to be one with another. Who you spend your time with is not something to leave to fate and cannot be a footnote on your ever-growing to-do list. It has to be a part of the plan. Like doing laundry—who you *do* has to be a part of your master plan.

There's a reason the cruelest punishment in prison is being placed in a room alone with no connection to the outside world. We are not created to be alone. Every success you encounter in life, whether getting to lead the new account at work or mastering the family chocolate cake recipe, is a result of your relationships with others and yourself. Recognizing the significance of love and relationships positions us for a fulfilled life.

Own Your Want for Love

Prioritizing relationships starts with embracing your want for love. I'm sure I got on my mama's last nerve as a little girl with all of my "I can do it." Tying shoestrings. Picking out clothes. Serving my plate. I was that little girl who always wanted to do everything for herself. That quality is still kicking in the woman I am now. So accepting the vulnerability of falling in love and willingly giving someone else the power to impact my life was a process. I had to realize sharing my space and heart (and food!) added to my life. It didn't take away from my ability to do for myself. Instead, being in love added amazing support and comfort to chase my dreams.

With many of my clients, one of the first hurdles is for them to proudly claim they want love. As accomplished women, admitting our desire for a strong relationship at first can feel like admitting weakness. But recognizing your own greatness and wanting to share that is not being thirsty. There's no shame in wanting to build something bigger than yourself. It takes strength to be soft and courage to acknowledge we could do it all but we don't want to. We are all naturally programmed to connect with others and discover love. Embrace your innate desire for lasting love.

Say it: I want love. I want to be loved and fully love another.

———

In coaching many career women to get out of their own way in the dating world, I have discovered the top phrases to leave behind when ready for a promotion in your love life.

1. Phrase to leave behind: "Men are intimidated by my career."
This is one of the biggest myths about today's men. After interviewing hundreds of guys, I've been pleasantly surprised to discover that most want a partner in life and not a passenger. They want to root for a woman pursuing her goals and also feel supported. What they don't want is a woman who defines herself by her job or reminds him she doesn't need a man in her life. So along with sharing your professional passions on a date, be sure to share your personal interests and the whole you.

2. Phrase to leave behind: "My guy is the only thing missing from my life."
Though finding a compatible guy should be a priority if you want a life partner, it is not a to-do item that will be checked off. Do not approach dating as a position you are looking to fill in a company. Being in a relationship will require your continued attention and commitment. And your life can be fulfilling regardless of your relationship status. The more you are happy with your life, the higher quality of daters you will attract.

3. Phrase to leave behind: "I want love to happen organically."
This is my top phrase I encourage Boss Brides to banish. Your dream guy is probably not going to spot you across the street, stop traffic, almost get hit, walk in front of you, and say you are the woman he's been waiting for his whole life as cars speed by. And that's okay. One thing I do with my coaching clients is ask them about a career highlight. Their eyes light up as they tell me about something incredible they pulled off and we write it all down. From buying houses to writing books and starting businesses, these women have done amazing things. With that burst of energy from reflecting on achieving a goal, I have them check in to the effort they put in for the results and

remind them that discovering lasting love will require some of that same faith, muscle, and commitment. Just because you meet the love of your life by asking your friends to set you up or strategically head to conferences full of the type of guy you want to date doesn't make the connection any less magical or your bond any less fulfilling. Getting the love you want requires casting your net as wide as possible to meet your match.

4. Phrase to leave behind: "Right now I'm just really busy with work." There's a lot of "should I call," "what do I wear," and "what the hell does this text mean" on the quest for love. With the uncertainty of dating, for many women it's easier to focus on a sure thing—your work. But this is a big mistake as your job will never hug you back and a few frogs are so worth it when you find your prince. When I spoke with New York psychologist and dating coach Paulette Murphy, PhD, she shared how the importance of finding a partner hit her at the beginning of her career. "When I was doing my residency, I noticed early on that when people are dying nothing mattered more than their significant other and family," she says. Investing in relationships and people is vital to your long-term health and happiness. And recent studies also show that an active dating life can increase productivity at work. Double win.

Career Confession

Actress and film producer Tangi Miller starred as smart and chic Elena on *Felicity*. As she continued to rise in her career, she noticed the trend of women being super-focused on their work, and then looking up to see they had climbed the ladder of success but not invested energy into their personal lives. She realized she was becoming one of them. The importance of being just as invested in your personal life as you are in your career hit her when she heard an unforgettable wedding story. "My friend went to a wedding of a professionally successful and sophisticated woman I knew. The lady told her family and friends that she was about to get married. People bought wedding dresses, family came to town, she had bridesmaids . . . and there was no groom. She was so together and you never would have thought things would turn out like that. That story stayed with me."

Her reality: "In my life, love wasn't on my list. It was, 'I want to go to this country,' 'I want to do this,' but love was nowhere to be found. And of course, if you don't put it out there it's certainly not going to happen. I've had actresses say to me, 'I just thought it would happen, and it never happened and I'm fifty and I don't want it to happen to you.' It's a real thing. It's wonderful to grow with somebody and find a life partner, and it takes planning for it."

Many Boss Brides are using the smarts from their professional lives to get the guy. I recently went to a wedding of one of my male friends. I was surprised how candid he was of her desire to lock him down. She was clear on her desire to be with him from the beginning and patiently waited until he came around. I'm sure there was someone who played it cool jumping for her bouquet.

Discover Your Dating Personality

It's time to get clear on your dating style to get a grasp of where you are now and how you can get to where you want. From speaking with hundreds of women on their dating and relationship habits, I've discovered six common love personalities. Complete the sentence below.

On a typical Friday night you can catch me . . .

A) On a date, duh. Finding Mr. Right takes regular auditions.

B) Looking through Facebook and googling the new guy I met. Can't be too careful.

C) Watching my fave rom-com on Netflix. They don't make the classics like they used to.

D) Taking advantage of the quiet in the office to get a little more work done. It's hustle season.

E) Hanging with one of my male best friends. Hoping tonight is the night he makes a move.

F) Asking out the cutie I messaged first on Match.com.

After choosing the answer that most matches you, read the corresponding letter below to discover your love personality. If you are in a relationship, think on your single days or your actions inside your current coupledom. You may have had trouble picking or feel torn between more than one, which is fine. We are all multidimensional. Read all descriptions that match to get more insight on your dating style.

A) The Serial Dater
Variety is the spice of your love life. You like the adventure of dinner with Cedric and a movie with Adam. Comparative shopping is your man strategy and quantity helps you discern quality. You enjoy the excitement of dating and new romance. And before you completely cut off a guy, you have his replacement lined up.

B) The Skeptic
You knew it. No one with those dimples and a VP title really had a "cousin" in town for the weekend. You are always on the search for what the latest guy is hiding. It may take two dates or two years, but you usually find a reason why he isn't "the one."

C) The Romantic
You are ready to be swept off your feet and begin your happily ever after with a Reem Acra gown. The "You complete me" scene in *Jerry Maguire* still makes you teary. You prefer to meet men while you are out and about instead of being set up because you want an awesome

"how we met" story for your 2.5 kids. Even though you don't know how half a baby actually works, you like the sound of "2.5."

D) The Career Queen

You have goals and are on track to achieve them! Your focus is mostly work with little time for play. Your personality gearshift is often stuck in work mode so your dates feel more like interviews.

E) First Lady of the Friend Zone

The relationship with a guy you like usually settles into platonic city and never ventures down romance drive. You are like one of the guys, but cute, and can't figure out why he doesn't see you are perfect partners.

F) The Role Reverser

You aren't afraid to take charge in your love life. You often make the first move from asking a guy out to letting him know when you are ready to get physical. You enjoy feeling in control in your relationships. You attract men who are enamored by your power.

The Serial Dater

YOUR SUPERPOWER

Courage. You are not afraid to put yourself on the dating scene and know that creating a great relationship will take effort on your part. You don't let what happened last week or rejection stop you from trying again.

YOUR BLIND SPOT

Creating a strong relationship takes time and requires you be all in. If your ultimate goal is ONE relationship with your soul mate, having so many choices can be overwhelming and actually makes it harder for you to assess a situation. Every relationship requires work. Get clear on your real objective and make the best choice. As the quote goes, one amazing husband in your bed is still better than two sexy suitors in the bush.

YOUR SUCCESS STRATEGY

Remember that quality beats quantity. Balance your openness to love with real focus on what you actually want. Check out the Check Your Checklist in the next chapter to hone what you are looking for. Your time and energy are finite and should be used wisely.

The Skeptic

YOUR SUPERPOWER

Knowledgeable. Your need for confirmation and security save you from heartache with anyone who has a sketchy past. You don't have a lot of breakup baggage because you don't let that many people close.

YOUR BLIND SPOT

Your lack of trust has you searching for "What's wrong" in just about every scenario. Being cautious is smart. Expecting doom is not and has you missing out on the power of love and the joy of falling for someone. The truth is the person you trust the least isn't someone else. It's you.

YOUR SUCCESS STRATEGY

Let it go. Whatever situation or circumstance rocked your trust in people is running the show and blocking great love. Know that your future can be bright and it will require you to let go and believe. Trust that everything will work out in the end.

The Romantic

YOUR SUPERPOWER

Optimism. Your belief in love is refreshing in an often cynical world. You know that love can change everything and is worth it. Love is indeed magical when you let it flow.

YOUR BLIND SPOT

The road to disappointment is paved with expectations. Your fantasies about how love should look may cloud the beauty of your own great love story. Let go of what a relationship should look like and grasp the life experiences you want with a soul mate. Life won't always be rosy and you want a real person to stand by you when life gets rocky. That's when love is its most powerful.

YOUR SUCCESS STRATEGY

Turn off the movies and lighten up on the romance novels to see beautiful love stories in the real world. Connect with couples you admire in real life to get a holistic look at love and all its complexities.

The Career Queen

YOUR SUPERPOWER

Driven. You are ambitious and achieve your goals. You aren't afraid to grind and have worked hard to get to where you are. The world is yours for the taking.

YOUR BLIND SPOT

Breaking news: No matter how hard you work, your job will never love you back. It's the people that make life worthwhile.

YOUR SUCCESS STRATEGY

The same muscle and focus you put into your professional life you can put into your personal life to have the relationship you crave.

First Lady of the Friend Zone

YOUR SUPERPOWER

Connected. You know men more than most women. A lot of your close friends are guys and you understand the ways the opposite sex operates.

YOUR BLIND SPOT

You've been so busy hanging with the guys you have not fully embraced what makes you a woman.

> ### YOUR SUCCESS STRATEGY
> Feed your innate femininity. This is not about what you wear but how you feel in your own body. You have to find your sexy before anyone else can.

The Role Reverser

YOUR SUPERPOWER
Secure. You know who you are, you see what you want and go for it. You are unapologetic and not afraid of rejection.

YOUR BLIND SPOT
Making the first move doesn't mean you don't have to let others in. Real relationships require authenticity and vulnerability on both parts.

YOUR SUCCESS STRATEGY
Keep going for what you want and take all of you wherever you go. We are all human so leave the façade at home.

If you have trouble discovering your dating personality, think about how others would summarize you. What dater would your best friend or ex pick?

In Ignite Your Love Life, my online dating course for professional women, I ask attendees to describe how current or past partners would portray them in relationships.

Let me introduce you to Janet and Carla, who I worked with to decipher their love pattern. Janet is the girl who always finds herself as First Lady of the Friend Zone. She will like a guy, but instead of getting the girlfriend title she ends up as a friend. She doesn't get invites to meet the parents but calls to watch the game. Then there is Carla, who is a merger of The Serial Dater and The Romantic, turning every hookup into her pseudo hubby. Each woman wonders why she keeps getting the same results. As you probably have guessed, it's because they keep teaching different guys how to treat them the same way.

For Janet, she's adventurous and feels most comfortable showing off her outdoorsy side to hide the vulnerability just beneath the surface. Her first conversations scream, "I am not a punk!" sprinkled with her knowledge of football, which she hopes will show she would be a great girlfriend for most guys. Unfortunately her bravado sends the message that she is just like one of the guys and she ends up treated as such. Instead of candlelight dinners, she gets details of how he's wining and dining the next chick.

For Carla, she's used to being in a relationship and takes the habits of a longtime girlfriend into casual encounters. Her casual fling got a Christmas present and invites to her dinner parties. The guys usually enjoy how much care she puts into the situationship, then are sobered by the fact that she is the type you build something with, and things fizzle.

In both instances men are taking their cues from these ladies on how they are to be treated. We've got Jane the homie and Carla the wife. Your turn:

- How are you usually treated while dating?
- What signals are you sending for this?

The Ring: Discuss Your Personality

The people who can probably best assess how you love and date are the people who have witnessed you dating. Call someone who has had a front row seat of your dating experiences to see which love personality they would say is you. It's no right answer, but great feedback if they see you in a way you don't see yourself.

I have found myself being all the love personalities at different points of my life. Recognizing what message we are putting into the world allows us to tweak it to receive what we are looking for. With my natural inclination to take charge in most instances, I was a Career Queen and a Role Reverser. A few years back I realized I was broadcasting "boss" in my professional life as well as in my personal relationships. I made a conscious effort to let more of my softer side out. I knew in the long run I didn't want to always be tasked with making decisions so realized I needed to cut back now, from picking the restaurant for brunch with my friends to deciding to always host my book club meetings. I could have learned the lesson earlier, had I taken a deeper look when my friends in high school called me "boss lady" after I somehow became the captain of most of our group projects. There is still a place to be the boss, but taking off the "I can do it" hat in my personal life and being more vulnerable has allowed me to get closer to the people I care about. Assessing your love personality allows you to better plan for the future you want. I have found a lot of professional women find themselves with Career Queen habits.

Identify Your Love Lifestyle

How we love is impacted by how we live. You may daydream about meeting men internationally during your travels around the world, but if you just started a three-year master's program, stolen kisses in Spain may be out of reach for a while. It's fine to fantasize on what you would like, as long as you keep a stiletto rooted in reality of the road to get there. Pose the following questions to yourself and write down the answers in the Boss Bride playbook (download your FREE interactive playbook at www.bossbride.com/playbook) to see how love already plays out in your life.

WHAT IS MY DATING DNA?

Like our physical genetics, our dating DNA is part nature and part nurture. Some things are an innate part of how you see the world and some are what you've learned from your parents and family. There is a reason all the dating reality shows bring on the parents of the contestants. They provide a peek into how you can be in relationships. Are healthy relationships in your family? Do you model your mom's knack to shut down during arguments or your dad's routine of bringing up the past? It's important to recognize the habits you have picked up and decide which to keep and lose.

HOW DO I SPEND MY WEEKENDS?

Take inventory of your free time to see what you are currently validating with your time and what gets your attention. Do you enjoy dancing with the girls or working on your side business? Are you spending the weekend regrouping from a job you hate? Also be honest about how you do what you do. Are you usually overbooked and rushing from brunch to get your dry-cleaned items?

WHAT AM I KNOWN FOR?

We are all known for something, whether it's being a straight shooter or fun flirt. Along with knowing yourself, it's important to be tuned in to how others view you. I realized my friends and men I've dated come to me for pep talks and have realized I don't attend pity parties. Sometimes I learn about challenges friends are having from someone else in our circle. And that's okay. Explore what friends and men come to expect from you.

WHO DO I CALL FOR GOOD AND BAD NEWS?

A big chunk of a strong relationship is the intimacy of letting someone else see the junk we would prefer to keep hidden. Identifying who you want to talk to in life's big moments allows you to see what, who, and how you let others into your life. Defining your confidantes also can help you discern what you look for to feel comfortable in sharing yourself.

WHAT ARE THE HATS I WEAR?

In looking to expand the love quotient in your life, it's important to see what's already there. Are you in charge of the office softball team or did you just join a book club? Do you spend half of your vacation days with family in Chicago? Get clear on how love fits in your life.

After deciphering your dating DNA, seeing how you spend your time and who you spend it with, summarize your love lifestyle and look for the areas you want to strengthen. Knowing how you love is powerful. I worked to check some of my baggage from past encounters before entering my last relationship. I then got checked by the impact of my dating DNA two years into dating him. Over brunch in Washington, DC, my god sister and I were catching up and of course the conversation went to our love lives. She told me how she and her boyfriend had gone through a rough patch and she asked him if he wanted to take a break. My then boyfriend was also dealing with some personal issues at the time and I had posed the same question to him. I thought about how our mothers, who are best friends, were women who left men who weren't doing right by them. I realized the impact that being raised by these strong women has had on us throughout our lives, including being open to walking away sooner than later if a relationship wasn't going the way we wanted. I also realized my default response is to run, so it's important for me to be clear I am leaving for the right reasons in a relationship and not just out of habit.

Get the Goal: "I Love Me"

While preparing for your future, enjoy this special time in your life! Along with love goals, I also ask my coaching clients to define three individual short-term goals they want to complete and challenge you to do the same. One woman shared she would ideally get married in five years, and before marriage she would like to learn another language, live in another country, and get her master's degree. She obviously had plenty to do to accomplish those goals, instead of wasting time worrying about a date for Friday night. Along with your long-term love goals identify your "I love me" goals that might be more challenging to accomplish with a serious relationship and family.

Sometimes we can be so focused on what we don't have, we miss what we do. Not waking up to your dream man on a Saturday morning may be the perfect time to take that yoga class you've been eyeing—and another way to meet new people. The time of "just doing me" can be fleeting, so soak up the chance for spontaneous adventures and whims.

Prepare for Love

It was a Sunday afternoon in Harlem. I was perched in the packed balcony of First Corinthian Baptist Church alongside a mix of international tourists, young professionals now making the area home, and folks who had been in the neighborhood for generations. Pastor Mike, our brilliant, funny, and grounded leader who easily transitioned from jeans to three-piece suits, came to the stage. He began the day's message with a story of his daughter. She loved the ocean when she was little and every time she saw a beach on TV she begged her parents to take her. Finally summer arrived, and they decided to grant the little girl her wish and travel to the shore. She was happy the entire ride. When they made it to the beach she got out of the car and took off running down the sand. She finally made it to the water! But when the waves started to come out, she turned around and ran just as fast away from the beach she had begged to see. After all her pleading to visit, she was scared. The idea of the ocean at home was great, but up close it was overwhelming.

Like most people, I have felt those conflicting emotions of wanting something, then being afraid when it actually shows up. For many daters, instead of waves, the want and unexpected fear are love and a strong relationship. Something we crave yet keep a safe distance away. Well, Boss Bride, let's make sure you are ready to get off the shore of your dreams. Check out these four habits to prepare for your someone special.

SET THE STANDARD

Begin now doing the things and going to the places you would with a partner. Daydream of traveling the world with your beau? Don't wait until he comes along to start filling your passport with stamps. When he does show up, you will already be in your groove and able to show instead of tell him about the life you want.

CONSIDER YOUR CIRCLE

Most people have a cousin or friend who can find the bad in anything. This is the friend who says, "I knew it," to every relationship that goes south. Even though we love these people, we have to limit our time with them so that outlook doesn't rub off. Be mindful of who you keep around you.

SECURE A LOVE BUDDY

Find someone who is also serious about being open to love. Share your goals and commit to keeping each other motivated and updated on your progress. There's nothing like a weekly call on your love life to keep you pushing to achieve your goals, and maybe sauntering across the room to make the first move.

SURROUND YOURSELF WITH THE LIFESTYLE

If you fantasize about a strong marriage, it's important to regularly see happily married couples. Along with real people, check out movies, magazines, websites, and other resources to normalize your happily ever after. See my favorites in the final chapter.

Build Your Relationship Muscle

Your professional skills do not magically transfer to being great in romantic relationships. Most of us have never taken a single class on how to be in a relationship. Trial and error can leave our most precious possession, our heart, bruised and battered. Yes to picking up this book! You can continue to learn with courses and resources at www .bossbride.com.

While preparing for a relationship, one of the students in my Ignite My Love Life course realized she wasn't all the way ready to share her space. After getting her career to where she wanted it and hearing her biological clock get a little louder (Her words: "I feel my eggs starting to dry up!"), she was ready and hoping for a serious relationship that led to more.

With her own starting five of men to take her out, meeting guys wasn't the problem. But wanting to actually share her time and space with someone? An issue. She'd gotten so used to doing her own thing and having the place to herself, she was looking at her watch and ready to show any suitor the door before the nightly news started.

So, she developed a plan to prepare for being in a relationship: get a dog.

My eyes lit up with this revelation. She then filled me in how a dog was the perfect prep for a boyfriend and how it will make her more warm and affectionate. She also had her top choices for type of dog and the qualities he needed to have (must fit in purse) and had friends who had rebounded from depression by getting a dog.

I congratulated her on being honest enough with herself to realize she wasn't totally open to the intimacy she craves. That's not easy. I also wished her well, if this was what she really wanted. But later that night I wondered if Madame Fifi will become another reason the new guy can't come over.

If the real issue is wanting to build stronger connections with the opposite sex, then that's where her focus has to be. A dog can be a beautiful part of your life and more and more studies prove how smart they really are. But I have yet to meet the dog that can rub your feet or make pancakes on Saturday morning.

Prepare to Be Intimate

Yes, I'm the girl at work who gives out vibrators. But true intimacy is not about taking our clothes off, but letting someone inside our hearts. Once I realized the residue and pain I had left from my parents' divorce, I began to see the ways I never expected to be supported.

Loving another person means allowing them to see all of who you are.

In my previous relationship, I took our intimacy to a new level a few weeks into dating. We were fully clothed and I was having a snotty cry. I had gotten up that morning ready to help someone else. There was a bone marrow drive to find a match for Jasmina Anema, a six-year-old battling leukemia. As a survivor of Hodgkin's lymphoma, a highly treatable cancer of the lymph nodes, I felt especially connected to her and woke up excited to help. Soon after arriving at the drive's location, I realized I might have come for nothing. Big signs said anyone with a cancer past could not be tested. I felt incredibly helpless. I headed back uptown and stopped by my boyfriend's apartment. I hadn't yet told him about my past illness and wasn't planning to share that day. Though I was proud to be a survivor, I wasn't quite ready to reveal that to someone I had just fallen in love with. To see the sympathy. To see the what-ifs of my health and that of my future kids. But a few minutes after arriving, he could sense something wasn't right and asked what was wrong. It was like a dam burst and I started crying and telling him about my past with cancer and the day's event at the drive for Jasmina. I also told him my new reality of possibly having kids of my own one day and not being able to help them if they needed medical assistance. We prayed for Jasmina. And he reminded me the same way everyone came out for Jasmina, if it were my child, God would provide. Sadly, while Jasmina found a donor, she passed away a few months later. I know she's fabulous in a special place and I continue to pray for her mom and all those she touched. I'm thankful for the short life she had on this earth.

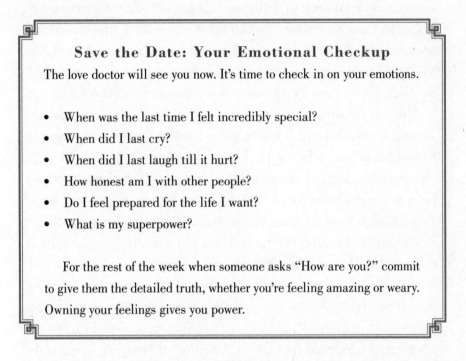

Save the Date: Your Emotional Checkup

The love doctor will see you now. It's time to check in on your emotions.

- When was the last time I felt incredibly special?
- When did I last cry?
- When did I last laugh till it hurt?
- How honest am I with other people?
- Do I feel prepared for the life I want?
- What is my superpower?

For the rest of the week when someone asks "How are you?" commit to give them the detailed truth, whether you're feeling amazing or weary. Owning your feelings gives you power.

Minding our emotions helps us stay in touch with our own joy and identifying people and experiences that make us feel good and bad.

Building lasting love asks us to let others see the real us, knowing every part of it is beautiful and sacred, even our pain and scars.

I have built a muscle by being more honest in my relationships, which allows people to feel connected to me and allows me to be free to be my authentic self. If I didn't have a good day, I didn't have a good day. Because I love on my scars, others do too.

#BossBride Vow

- I vow to let all of me be loved. I vow to honor and not hide how I feel.

Check Your Focus

Growing up in Atlanta, my ballet and tap teacher was the amazing Ms. Michelle. I was infatuated with this tall, ballsy woman who owned and operated the popular dance studio in my neighborhood. And Ms. Michelle's biggest tip for twirls was the same as most dance teachers': Be careful where you spot because it is where you will end up.

She was referring to what we focused on when we started to spin across the room because it was exactly where we landed. Not paying attention before you started to twirl led you on the wrong path and made you dizzy. For some of us, we are twirling through life focused on our singleness and what we don't have, then wonder why we are perpetually alone or not having the things we want. Well, it's what you are spotting.

Commit to focus on the life and love you want. If every Saturday is spent at the salon and then brunch with your girls discussing the lack of men, reconsider what you are spotting and how you are spending your time. Try new activities and discussions on ways to meet new people with friends in healthy relationships, instead of focusing on what hasn't happened for you yet. Be mindful how you define yourself. If your goal is to be in a relationship, don't brand yourself as "the single girl." I've lost count of the number of blogs with "single" in the title that talk about the want for a relationship. Start today being the you of the future. Our mind is the most powerful part of our bodies. Our thoughts and words manifest into actions and habits that define our lives. By focusing on the good things we want in life, they begin to come into our world. You have the power to magnetize your thoughts to you. Make sure that they are positive and progressive.

Long before *The Secret* hit bookstores a lot of us already knew the key to getting what you want was believing it would come to pass. Since moving to New York I have been vocal that this city is one of the best to be a single woman hoping to meet a great guy, much to the sighs of many women and friends. I've met my share of f*ck boys and am not saying hot and thoughtful guys are hanging from the trees, but there are still many good guys around. Believing good men exist isn't a guarantee a great one will show up tomorrow, but having faith is half the battle. It also means you won't be shocked when things happen just like you hoped. When those experiences do come, enjoy the moments instead of missing the value of today by worrying about the future. Believing you deserve love and being open to the many ways it may show up is an essential part to receiving it.

My friend Fawn Weaver found that out firsthand. While working as a business manager for an LA hot spot, she went to get her hair done at her regular salon. She didn't have her laptop and cell phone like she usually did so for once she had time to chat with the salon owner while getting styled. "I want to be a great wife," she found herself saying. They talked some more and she headed back to work. Later Fawn learned that after she left the stylist called her son and said, "I just met your wife." A month later the couple connected, four months later he proposed, and eight months after their first date they said "I do." Fawn stayed committed to her goal to be a great wife and created the Happy Wives Club community of more than a million women in 110 countries to celebrate marriage. And it all started from simply saying her desires out loud at the hair salon.

How we treat ourselves will also shape how other people treat us. If you pick up the phone for your new guy who only calls after 11:00 p.m., he will keep on calling with your consent. If I keep saying yes to last-minute invites, they will continue to come in. We often have to teach people how to treat us. Before you open your mouth, your actions are saying plenty on how you expect to be treated. I've had many doors opened for me and my hand kissed because I politely let that expectation be known without a word. I am the queen of an "excuse me?" to the rude customer service rep or the flighty waiter as I kindly remind them that's not how you talk to me. I also love on myself so the man I'm with knows how I like to be treated. I continue to make plans and do the things I enjoy, letting him know I may not always be available on a whim and appreciate when he makes plans in advance. Our efforts of establishing ourselves and what we like is not only good for us, but can be a turn-on for men.

You've Got the Power

Here's the inside scoop some men hope we never realize: We have the power in relationships. We say more than yes to a dress, and decide things from whether there is a first date to when things get sexual.

With the headline-grabbing "man shortage" some women are feeling the pressure to move quickly, forgo commitment, or deal with more than they should. And many guys have gotten spoiled by us giving up way too much.

If all women said we wouldn't have sex with a man until at least the fifth date, we'd all benefit and be giving each other head nods on the way to dinner. Historically, one of the reasons people got married younger was to have sex. It was understood that in order to get some, men would have to put a ring on it. It's a personal choice if you decide to wait for marriage to enjoy your natural sexual urges. Celibacy has netted results and healthy relationships for many couples (check out the book *The Wait* by dope husband and wife duo DeVon Franklin and Meagan Good to learn more, and you'll see a quote from yours truly on the back cover). Either way, women hold power in relationships, which goes far beyond sex.

BOSS BRIDE CONFESSIONS
WORKING WIFE CONFESSION

New York psychologist Paulette Murphy, PhD, knows all about being submerged in your career yet yearning for love. When she was ready for someone special, she took her hustle to her personal life, committing to do one thing each day that would get her closer to meeting her life partner. She now uses the lessons she learned along with her professional knowledge.

INVEST IN LOVE

When I was single, I felt I would never find a guy because I was working so hard. So I decided to do one thing a day to widen my circle, whether it was research an event or ask friends for referrals. That was my time just for me each day. One day I emailed a friend who said he knew a great guy and that guy is now my husband of six years. If you want to find the right relationship, you have to make the time.

USE MARRIED WOMEN AS MATCHMAKERS

Married women will try and match women we like with nice men we know. We make great wing women and don't mind talking a man up a storm, so ask your friends to pick a weekend to go on a manhunt with you.

Get Inspired in Love!

Visualizing your goals allows you to see clearly the desires of your heart and develop the focus to get there. Creating a vision board is such a freeing experience to allow yourself to dream without limitations on what you can and can't do. It forces us to break out those fantasies we sometimes keep tucked away.

CREATE

Use old magazines and catalogs to clip photos and quotes that inspire you and embody your love and life goals. Cute couples and professional women are all mainstays on my boards. Smiling babies have also started being added. Be sure to get your favorite couples and she-roes who inspire you, whether your own family and friends or famous "friends" in your head. Include personal notes and mementos like the card from the first time you got roses at the job. Also get a photo of you from one of your happiest moments to remember that feeling. I type up my favorite quotes and search online for photos I can't easily find to personalize my boards. Once complete, you can put it in a nice frame or tape it to your wall guerrilla-style like me.

CONSUME

The most important part of the vision board process is to put it in a place you will often see it, even if it's only briefly each day. Those seconds help to keep your goals top of mind and for your actions to follow your heart. Hot spots are next to your bed, mirror, on the back of the door, or even in the bathroom. You can also take your vision on the road. Snap photos of your vision board and use it as a screensaver for your phone or computer. From the planner and compact in your purse to your desk at work, post inspiring photos and quotes that remind you of your passion and goal.

Save the Date: Declare Your Love Goals

Now that you have crystalized your desires for relationships, it's time to declare to the universe when you will achieve them. Adding deadlines to our goals makes us accountable and urgent. You don't have to have all the details of how it will happen, but trust that it will.

As I first toyed with writing this book, I was a social media specialist discussing fashion and beauty during the day. I taped a picture of Boss Bride Beyoncé and her husband, Jay-Z, on my office computer to remind me each day of my true mission to serve a new generation of women. A few years earlier at my first job out of college, I had a picture of a grinning Nelson Mandela on my wall so no matter what happened during the day, I had no excuse not to smile if he could be full of joy after being wrongly jailed for twenty-seven years.

With a clear vision of what you want, be open to the many ways it may arrive. Keisha Omilana is living proof of the unexpected ways love can show up. It was the busiest time of the year for the professional model: New York Fashion Week. On the heels of her national ad campaign with Pantene, she was standing outside the train station in New York's Union Square frantically talking to her Ford Models agent because she was late to a casting. Kunle Omilana was walking by when she caught his eye. He watched her and patiently waited half an hour for the call to end. He then introduced himself, said she was the most beautiful woman he'd ever seen, and asked her out. She declined, made up a fake boyfriend (one of the single Boss Bride's favorite weapons), and ran down the train station stairs.

"My woman's intuition said go back," she says. "And when I did he was there waiting and told me 'This is the best decision you have ever made.'" It turned out to be just that. "I knew he was special on our first date. He had rose petals leading to our table and looked in my eyes the whole night." The attention had her so unsettled she remembers knocking everything off the table. He wasn't deterred and said, "You are going to be my princess."

Nigerian Prince Kunle had come to New York from London to find his bride. Yes, the real-life version of *Coming to America*. Princess Keisha had no clue he was royalty until she met his family shortly before he proposed. She was happy to find a man who celebrated her success. "The first thing he loved about me is that I was driven, independent, and a career girl." Now the two are happily married with a son and daughter, and run the Wonderful brand. This princess and Boss Bride knows that fairy tales can come true—no fake boyfriend necessary.

In my relationships workshops, I always share how my man mojo of guys approaching me is extra strong on my birthday and as soon as I get into a relationship. As soon as I was off the market, it seemed like a dam had burst and a lot of guys were trying to make their move on the train, on the street, and my favorite man hot spot, the airport. *Where was this abundance when I was single?* I wondered after politely declining one cutie. It wasn't that they could sniff out a man close to my heart. They simply could sense my joy and happiness and wanted some of whatever I was sipping on.

Your Relationships Rule Your Life

I thought this book would be coming out as the first woman sat in the Oval Office in the White House as president of the United States. Secretary of State Hillary Clinton lost the electoral college (yes, she won the popular vote). And the outcome was directly impacted by relationship decisions.

I wore my royal-blue pantsuit with a Michelle Obama T-shirt to the polls to vote for a woman for president. I was heading inside Javits Center with the crowds when it dawned on me I didn't like crowds. So I left with plans to attend a friend's election party. It had been a month since I met Sir Brooklyn and we hadn't seen each other since. I invited him to the election party. He suggested we meet for a drink first to catch up. We met in Dumbo, Brooklyn, and had a drink while the election played out. I was perplexed as Secretary Clinton started to lose states. He could tell I was starting to worry and suggested we go for a walk. We did. We held hands and underneath the Brooklyn Bridge we had our first kiss. While in my blue pantsuit. We went to another bar to see if the unexpected election result was happening. It was. We did not elect a Madame President.

A few weeks after the harrowing election I visited my cousin's house and *Weiner* was playing, the documentary following Anthony Weiner, the disgraced congressman who mistakenly tweeted a picture of his bulge instead of a direct message to a college student while his wife, Huma Abedin, was pregnant with their son. Yeah, that guy. Huma is Hillary Clinton's right hand, top aide, and was vice chair of her presidential campaign. And like many women with a hectic career, Huma's dating life intertwined with her job. While at the Democratic National Committee retreat on Martha's Vineyard in 2001, she met then-congressman Anthony Weiner. It was Hillary's first summer as a senator.

Huma first blew him off but over time their paths continued to cross and they started to date. In 2010 former president Bill Clinton presided over their wedding ceremony.

The film shows how Weiner tries to restart his political career in 2013 and is running for New York City mayor after the sexting scandal. The documentary gets increasingly uncomfortable as we witness more explicit texts from Weiner as he clamors to lead the capital of the world. We watch Huma stand close by as he comes clean on more pics to more women and the increased strain on their marriage as the cameras roll. He loses the mayoral campaign.

And this Weiner may have cost us our first female president.

In an unprecedented move, a few weeks before the 2016 election FBI Director James Comey sent a letter to Congress saying the FBI had found new emails to review on how Secretary Clinton handled classified information. This was after he had already closed the investigation on her, so it put a dark cloud over her shortly before voters headed to the polls. Following the election, Clinton stated Comey's letter had a direct impact on voters and her not winning the electoral college to become president.

And where did those new emails Comey reported about come from?

Anthony Weiner's computer. Less than three months before the election Anthony Weiner was exposed for more sexting with women and it was worse than before: he was back to sending pictures of his bulge, this time as the couple's young son slept nearby in one of the photos. It covered newspapers and made headlines. Huma finally had enough and separated from her husband just a few weeks before the election, the biggest time of her career.

"After long and painful consideration and work on my marriage, I have made the decision to separate from my husband," Huma Abedin said in a statement.

Things got even worse a month after the scandal broke when it was revealed that one of the women Weiner, fifty-one, was sending sexual texts to was a fifteen-year-old high school student. Investigators seized his laptop and found some emails between Huma and Hillary, giving Comey ammunition to publicly cast doubt on Clinton. Six weeks after the election the FBI began an investigation into the disgraced congressman for potentially preying on a minor.

Huma's choice in a husband impacted not only her life and career, but that of her mentor and boss.

Sadly, Weiner wasn't the first scandal of infidelity to hit Hillary Clinton. While first lady she forgave and decided to move forward with her husband, then-president Bill Clinton.

In her memoir, *Living History*, she talks about the moment Bill told her about his relationship with Monica Lewinsky, saying she was "dumbfounded, heartbroken and outraged."

> Gulping for air, I started crying and yelling at him. "What do you mean? What are you saying? Why did you lie to me?"

We can only imagine Clinton's anguish as her husband's indiscretions came to light in the White House. She stood by his side and he by hers as she continued a political career after his term as president, when she served as a U.S. senator, secretary of state, and ran two campaigns for president of the United States. How did they rebuild their marriage to get to a place where the first word in her Twitter bio is "wife"? The Clintons didn't talk about the low moments in their marriage during the campaign, possibly a missed opportunity to connect with voters, especially women.

Our decisions in who we date and love impact everything else in our lives. In the next chapter I break down how to discern if the guy you are dating has staying power.

One of the best things women can do for their career is to date with intention and discover a supportive partner. We've often heard beside every great man is a great woman, alluding to the impact the right woman has on a man's success. As women excel professionally, we are

seeing the same impact of a supportive partner to our rise to the top—
and staying there.

Even the global queen of media sometimes hits a wall. After twenty-
five years of motivating and empowering millions of women on her
legendary daytime talk show, Oprah Winfrey needed a sip of her own
feel-good juice in 2012. The "live your best life" cheerleader had hung
up the mic of her daily TV show after a historic twenty-five seasons. In
her sendoff, the world toasted her stellar run with a magical finale that
included Beyoncé, Tom Cruise, Madonna, and Will Smith. But her
high was soon served a dizzying low. Her new Oprah Winfrey Network
cable station struggled to gain its footing and ratings were far below
expectations after the channel first launched, a far cry from the magical days when she handed out cars like they were sticks of gum. The
self-made billionaire became a favorite headline as critics speculated
whether her golden touch had ended and if the channel would survive. "Oprah's got her OWN problems" shared the *Today* show while
the *New York Post* railed "Oprah Network Struggling So Badly It's
Come to This . . ."

Oprah powered on and made steps to steer the rocky channel into
steady waters, including appearing on many shows on the network.
While interviewing *Kony 2012* director Jason Russell for her show
Oprah's Next Chapter, she realized the symptoms he described of a
nervous breakdown were the same ones she was having. In her dark
hour the inspirational leader knew just whom she needed to turn to:
Stedman Graham, her life partner of more than twenty years. "He was
amazing," she told *People* magazine. "He said, 'You can't even think
about quitting. You have been in cruise control. It's gonna turn around,
but you've gotta do the work.'"

Graham's place as a centering force in the world of Winfrey is
quickly apparent. On the high-stakes last season of her daytime show,
he surprised her in hair and makeup on her more stressful days. And
as their more than twenty-year engagement proves, one of the secrets
to their successful relationship is not conforming their partnership to
society's standards. Their first date over twenty years ago is certainly

original. "We went waterskiing. Stedman tried twenty-eight times [to get up] and wouldn't give up," Oprah shares. "I thought, 'What is wrong with him? Good lord, this is exhausting!' He would not quit." That can't stop, won't stop mentality was the same message the motivational speaker and marketing entrepreneur used to encourage his lady to push through the tough start of her network. Now the channel has record ratings and continues to excel. In the dizzying world of entertainment, Oprah attributes her dazzling staying power to the anchor in her life: love. "We have what a lot of people have who have been in a relationship for a long time. We want each other to succeed," Stedman said. "I want her to be as successful as she possibly can. I encourage that. That's not always easy to do when you are a man in a relationship with a very powerful woman. I'm not threatened by her fame, or her success or her money. That's who she is. It doesn't have anything to do with how I define myself." I got to see Oprah and Stedman's love in person at her The Life You Want Tour stop in New Jersey (and at their home in California—but we will get to that in Chapter 8).

Coupled-Up Perks

Prioritizing love not only gets you closer to achieving your personal goals, but also helps your professional pursuits. A *Forbes* article reported that women are experiencing higher rates of career burnout than men. One reason offered is that men are more likely to do things for their personal well-being at work, helping to prevent burnout. Men are 25 percent more likely to take breaks during the day, 5 percent more likely to go to lunch, and 35 percent more likely to just relax. Getting active in your dating life is a constant reminder you are so much more than work.

Marriage provides benefits to women and children that cannot be duplicated in any other relationship. Here are some of the benefits attributed to marriage.

Married people:

- live longer
- have better health
- make more money
- accumulate more wealth
- enjoy increased well-being of children
- have better and more frequent sex

There are also lower incidences of domestic violence among married women and child abuse among children living with their biological parents. Marriage also reduces the chances that women and children will live in poverty.

Start Today

One of the biggest mistakes we make in life and love is believing we can put things off until tomorrow. Cancer forced me to prioritize love sooner than I expected. As I shared earlier, at nineteen I was diagnosed with cancer and underwent nine months of chemotherapy and radiation. I was very blessed to catch it early and had one of the most treatable cancers with a low chance of returning. But the experience allowed me to see tomorrow is not promised and to make the most of each day I have on this earth. I realized there was no time for fear, anger, or second-guessing. It made me more fearless as I pushed for things I had only daydreamed about before—from moving to New York to giving guys the sexy eye from across the room. What did I really have to lose? Recognizing the fallacy of tomorrow has been invaluable in my relationships as well. I am open and honest about how I feel and don't let anger fester. None of us can afford to waste valuable time thinking someone else will bring us our dreams. If you want someone to rub your feet in your fifties, plan now. If you want two kids by thirty-eight with four years between them, do what you can today to prepare yourself for your future. We have to take "tomorrow" off the table and remember all we have is today. And love is our number-one to-do item each and every day.

Whispers of a Woman
WHAT EACH WORKING WIFE WOULD SAY TO HERSELF AS SHE WALKED DOWN THE AISLE

Buckle up! **What I literally asked myself at the church door, before walking down the aisle: If nothing changes would you be happy? Thankfully the answer was yes.** Work it out and listen to your heart, not your head! **Be happy.** Trust your gut and stay true to who you are. Allow yourself to make mistakes and then learn from them. **Whatever life throws at us, we're gonna be in this together.** Do as much as you can with your husband before you have kids. Once you have kids, life changes for a long time. It's a good change but you won't be able to go on that African safari for a while. **Wait another year.** It may not be perfect all the time, but just keep moving forward. **Laugh through EVERYTHING!** Coming from a woman married so long, girl, it isn't going to be easy but make time for one another and don't sweat the small stuff. **You can have it all. You have to create a balance that does not leave anything neglected. You have to make sure to always remember to take care of you.**

3

DATE LIKE A PRO

Some people are settling down, some people are settling and some people refuse to settle for anything less than butterflies.
—CANDACE BUSHNELL,
AUTHOR OF *SEX AND THE CITY*

"sup"

That's what Eric's text said, trying to test the waters with my girl Joy.

They had been unofficially a couple—regular contact, steady sex—for more than a year. She had ended things three weeks before, tired of living in the gray zone.

"Not only does he not step up or pick up the phone to call, but he can't even cap the 's'?" said an exasperated Joy as we caught up one night.

Welcome to the modern dating scene. Many women feel ill prepared for an adulthood marked by a complicated dating pool, pressure to succeed at home and at work, casual sex, and social media and technology now shaping every part of our lives. Like my girl Joy, many women have found themselves less than satisfied and sometimes in "situationships," an almost relationship with regular interaction but no definition or commitment.

To have the love you deserve means taking full ownership of your happiness and setting your expectations (ahem, Joy, he did not deserve the benefits of a job he wasn't doing). We can bring the hustle we have in our careers to our personal lives to date like a pro. That's how women meet quality singles to build a lasting, fulfilling, committed relationship.

Relationships have changed more in the last fifty years than in the last five centuries before. Following the growth of opportunities for women and the digital explosion, today's woman is unlike any before her and she is building her own happiness in a whole new world. I've seen the transformation up close as a speaker at iDate in Las Vegas and the Europe Dating Awards conference in Amsterdam, bringing together dating industry professionals from all over the world.

Our generation didn't invent complicated relationships, though our issues are exasperated by changing social norms. Today, would-be players are exposed by Facebook status updates instead of nosy neighbors. Couples meet—and break up—online, and her girls, his crew, and both of their mamas feel free to add their two tweets to the drama. You discover the winter boo is a wrap when his new lady tags him in photos from their Miami getaway.

With all the ways we have to communicate—telephone, Twitter, text, Facebook, Google Hangouts, DM, WhatsApp, email—somehow we can still be unclear on the message. Psychologist Tiffany D. Sanders, PhD, noticed the impact of technology on our dating lives. "With the rise of social media there is a decline in actual social skills," she says. "How do I get to know you if we only communicate via text? Dating today is a challenge and women are kissing and texting a lot more frogs to get to a good guy."

Although our dating rituals are more fluid than in past generations, the end goal is the same. Most women still want to get married, according to the National Marriage Project. We just want to take our time to get it right, contributing to America's record-low marriage rates. Many singles are slowly easing toward the aisle after witnessing the breakup of their parents or other couples in childhood, as U.S. divorce rates peaked in the eighties and nineties.

The good news is there are enough great people on this planet for each of us to have the love we desire. The reality check is we will have to play an active role in receiving the love we deserve since most of us aren't marrying a high school sweetheart (unless he resurfaces on Facebook, is single, and still cute).

Love is our most powerful emotion.

And for centuries, it was not a reason to get married. While love has always been a primal emotion, it was not often viewed as a primary reason to marry. In fact in many cultures it was looked down on if a couple were deeply in love. Marriage was a business decision to set yourself up for the best opportunity to survive.

Couple Habits Through History

In *Marriage, A History* researcher Stephanie Coontz breaks down the many ways people have dated and mated through time:

- In the Middle Ages the French defined love as a "derangement of the mind" that could be cured by sexual intercourse, either with a loved one or with a different partner.

- A woman in ancient China might bring one or more of her sisters to her husband's home as backup wives.

- Eskimo couples often had cospousal arrangements, in which each partner had sexual relations with the other's spouse.

- In Tibet and parts of India, Kashmir, and Nepal, a woman may be married to two or more brothers, all of whom share sexual access to her. Among the brothers, sexual jealousy is rare.

- In many working-class communities in Cameroon, too much love between husband and wife is seen as disruptive because it encourages the couple to withdraw from the wider web of dependence that makes the society work.

- In Europe, during the twelfth and thirteenth centuries, adultery became idealized as the highest form of love among the aristocracy.

So much of the past ways we mated were because men held the power in society, especially when it came to financial resources. The hard fight for women's empowerment has changed the game drastically. As our professional opportunities have grown, so have our expectations for our relationships. Since we don't need a man to cover our bills, our hierarchy of needs have moved up to desiring someone with whom we connect mentally, emotionally, spiritually, and sexually, and hopefully gets the approval of our family and friends. And not all places in the world are taking a modern approach to marriage. When I had a relationships blog I got a pitch from a woman in India who wanted to share her radical love story: She had married for love, which was not the norm in a culture that still has arranged marriages.

Though we may raise our eyebrows at some of the mating habits of the past or of different societies, we definitely have our own dating routines that are distinct from those of any people before us. Here are just a few of the ways our dating lives are drastically different now.

1. Online dating is here to stay. It's okay to look, as Match.com, a leader in online dating, proclaims. The stigma around online dating has continued to erode and swipe apps like Tinder and Bumble have made it easier than ever to meet someone new. We use technology for everything else. Why not in our love lives? More than a third of couples marrying today met online.

2. Google the guy you're dating. Getting to know you speeds up pretty fast with each of us having a digital footprint unveiled with an online search. After meeting Sir Brooklyn and before our first phone call a week later, we'd both googled each other. I sang a hook from one of his songs. He commented on my Twitter followers and said, "You internet famous." Welcome to dating in the digital age.

3. Sex is. The modern invention of dependable contraception has taken some the pressure off our sex lives. (#ThxBirthControl! Explore new options at bedsider.org.) There's still the nervousness of first-time partners and letting this new person see you sans bra, but not the added question each time you've had intercourse if it will lead to a pregnancy. BYOCondoms. And know that the new guy probably watches some porn . . . And maybe you have a favorite site with more female-friendly porn options (I recommend MakeLoveNotPorn.com if you don't).

4. What are we? This question increasingly comes up with couples not technically in a committed relationship unless both of you have agreed to monogamy and are not dating anyone else or are active online. Don't be afraid to state up front what you want and keep relationship perks like sex and cooking to yourself until you have commitment. That's what my friend Joy learned the hard way.

5. You are sometimes Dutch. With gender roles continuing to evolve, men don't always have to pay for dates. It's cool to offer or pay for a date here and there, or offer to cover the tip to show a guy you aren't in it just for the free meals. As women, we also often get ourselves to and from dates.

6. Text me, tease me. Texting has created a new opportunity for sharing our feelings and so much else to analyze while dating with the influx of emoticons, Bitmoji, and memes. And texting makes it easy for a guy to ask for pics of your lady parts—and for him to send you the classic dick pic. You cannot unsend so tread lightly on the sexting.

7. Who's the daddy? DNA tests have transformed genealogy as a swab of the mouth can prove once and for all who is family, a very modern revolution.

Things have certainly evolved. The pressure to get hitched remains. Not only are family members asking about our marital plans, so are our coworkers and our social media feed. "I see engagement photos, wedding pictures, and proposal announcements almost daily on Facebook," said my college roommate Amber, in her mid-twenties. She reconnected with her boyfriend from senior year and a few years later became the woman with engagement and wedding pictures in my feed.

How we arrive at coupledom can vary by culture and location. After speaking at the Matchmakers and Dating Coaches Conference in New York, I got to mingle with dating experts from every continent.

After taking selfies with matchmakers from Japan, Peggy Wolman, a Boston grandmother turned professional cupid, told me to tell you to consider enlisting the older people in your life to help find a solid match. "We have time and we can read people," Aunt Peggy added. Universally, the most successful singles are embracing what makes them special and taking their personal lives seriously.

Since 2003, the Matchmaking Institute, founded by Lisa Clampitt, has certified more than fifteen hundred matchmakers from around the world. Here are some of the latest global dating trends:

- The United States is about five years ahead of the world on dating habits. Online dating and matchmaking are hot here and now growing in Europe and other areas.

- There is an abundance of fabulous women that are educated and successful worldwide, especially in Southeast Asia. (Hey Boss Brides!)

- In big cities around the world, there's so much choice. The more options you have the more challenging it can be to meet someone. We urge people to focus on their values and goals, go on dates with a handful of quality people, choose the best one and make it work. Don't overanalyze it for ten years. Do a lot of work in the beginning and create a relationship that is continually growing.

I have spent the last decade exploring how we date and mate. What got me here was a simple question: **"Have you met your husbands yet?"**

My friends and I were asked this by a dolled-up woman of a certain age with coiffed hair and a stunning shawl. We were editors for *The Hilltop*, our college newspaper founded by Zora Neale Hurston. The question was posed when we were in the restroom at the fancy alumni dinner Howard University hosts each year. I was twenty years old at the time and dumbfounded to be asked if I'd vetted a spouse before I could legally drink. She sensed our unease and followed up with "Well, you don't have to marry him yet. I met my neurosurgeon while in school and we married a few years later." She finished primping and sashayed out of the restroom. I rolled my eyes, thinking we were in school for an education, not scouting husbands. Did she not make it into the twenty-first century? Our job as women was not to simply find husbands. We had a chance to pursue our dreams and then find someone who could handle all of our amazingness, if that's what we wanted. As we walked back to the table my "Wasn't that weird?" morphed into "Oh shit. Is she on to something?" as I began to wonder if everyone was at school trying to find a partner while I studied and fantasized about a career in the media.

What I didn't know was that woman would change my life. Her question and my puzzlement came at the perfect time. I was in the middle of cheating on my senior thesis with episodes of *Flavor of Love* (I know). My adviser and career godmother Yanick Rice Lamb told me to find a topic that had me curious. And wondering if coeds in the early 2000s were looking for husbands had my eyes all the way open. Thus began my thesis: "State of Our Unions: Today's College Women—Working on a Bachelor's or Looking for a Bachelor."

I was knee deep in my research the next school year with surveys, interviews, and focus groups. Thankfully most college women I surveyed weren't stressed about finding partners and established married women did not encourage young women to be consumed with scouting spouses—though they did say remember to keep love on our radar.

I was also battling the worst senioritis. After a summer in New York interning at magazines and living in the city that sleeps on the train after a night out, I was over school and itching to be grown full-time. When my writing and reporting class required us to select a beat to write about for the semester, I chose dating, since I was already all up in everyone's love lives.

I could turn just about any topic into something about dating and relationships. As the Martin Luther King, Jr., holiday approached, I wondered if college women were interested in dating a man like Dr. King. I got a mix of responses, as some women liked the qualities he represented and others wanted a man who would have more time for them. Stereotypical millennials we could be.

What I didn't know was an interesting topic to explore after a random conversation in the bathroom would foreshadow my future and inspire my life's work. Four days after graduation—where Oprah Winfrey told us "your integrity is not for sale"—I moved to New York. The next day I was at my new cubicle working as an online editorial assistant for *Essence*, where I managed relationships content for the website. Within a year I was promoted to associate editor for the site and read all the emails and comments. Seeing the questions and stories from women about their dating lives made me want to continue to be a part of the solution. I trained as a relationships educator and began hosting workshops at the college level, including the campus of South Carolina State University, where my parents met. Their divorce was my motivation to help others get it right. I knew love was possible and would require work.

A few years later I was named relationships editor for *Essence*. One of my responsibilities was finding sexy and successful bachelors around the country for the brand's Single Man of the Month feature. We shined these fellas up with glamorous photo shoots and I pulled out their make-you-grin responses.

What I quickly learned was the woman who read my pages loved a mature, established man who had charm and humor, and of course made you look twice when you saw him. So when a tall, handsome, broad-shouldered business owner and author with a PhD slid into my inbox, I knew he was a fit. And his answers didn't disappoint.

His most romantic date: Once I surprised a woman with a day trip to Boston. I had flowers waiting for her when we arrived and we enjoyed the cuisine and history in a day. I'd love to visit Harlem for a day and enjoy Melba's soul food with someone special.

His secret weapon: After starting a soup kitchen at my church growing up, the older women taught me how to really cook. People love my fried turkey, greens, and peach cobbler.

Why he's ready for love: Our days are better when you have the person you are supposed to be with and I look forward to better days. I've taken my time for the right person. Men have a duty to be a protector for a wife and I take that seriously.

Didn't I warn you? Not only was he fine and smart, he could make peach cobbler. The readers loved him and emails poured in to the account we hosted for him. It was my responsibility to make sure every email sent in to him made it to his personal inbox. While forwarding emails one day, a sender's name caught my attention: Bernice A. King.

Was the baby girl of Dr. Martin Luther King, Jr., and Coretta Scott King writing a kind note to this bachelor? She was and I made sure the doctor got the email. Years before when I wrote about Dr. King and wondered if women wanted to date a guy like him, I could not have imagined this moment. I also had not thought about how being the daughter of such an icon impacted her own love life. I wanted to find out and reached out for an interview. She graciously said yes.

While home in Atlanta, I went to the King Center to meet Elder Bernice King a few days after Ava DuVernay and the cast of *Selma* stopped by. Dr. Martin Luther King, Jr., and Coretta Scott King were trailblazers of global change, dedicating their lives to civil rights and are an iconic example of love. For Bernice, they were also Mom and Dad.

Their portraits hang all around the center. I took in that these were real people who made real sacrifices while trying to raise their own family. Bernice was radiant as she welcomed me into her office and honestly opened up on how having such a public family impacted her romantic life. Here are some of her answers from our interview for *Essence*.

DADDY'S IMPACT

Like a lot of women, I hope to marry someone like my dad. My father just happens to be Martin Luther King, Jr. Being the daughter of a civil rights legend works for some areas, but hasn't always been a plus on the dating scene. I will probably never say to a man "You're just like my dad," because he was one of a kind. His spirituality, his intellect, and his commitment to changing the world are all traits I look for in the man I hope to one day marry. He loved a joke and was a great dancer.

LESSONS ON LOVE

I've seen marriage as an enduring commitment, and I take it very seriously after watching my mother be married to my father for life, even after he passed. My mother really wanted me to find someone before she died. She emphasized to my siblings and me that we should date, and ultimately marry, someone with similar values.

SEEKING HER ROYAL MATCH

In law school, I fell in love with Travis,* whom I met at a park. We almost got engaged after dating a few years. One day it hit me that the relationship wouldn't last. People used to tease and call Travis "Mr. King" and it bothered him. I realized I would need someone who would be ready for what a life with me would mean and who had already found success on his own. I have seen God's amazing ways of blessing us many times and am open to meeting my future husband in a nontraditional way. It has been quite a journey and I have faith my own king will show up at the appointed time.

*Name changed.

Bernice is definitely a Boss Bride, following her heart while pursuing her fullest potential. Though we are not all dating in the shadows of a civil rights icon, dating today can be complicated for many women. We can relate to seeking someone who shares our values and fully accepts all we bring to the table, without being intimidated.

Dating as a Powerhouse

As a powerful woman, it is so important you discover a man that is emotionally mature. Who realizes he is more than his work and doesn't subscribe to outdated thinking rooted in patriarchy that a man has to make the most money and run the show. Your stock will only continue to rise and it is important you have someone who is your cheerleader and does not see you as a competitor.

In my interviews with hundreds of women, I found most successful and happily married women have a spouse that falls in one of these categories: a companion, a partner, or a provider.

A companion: someone who joins you on your journey and gives you the space to work independently. They have a clearly defined role in your personal life separate from your career.

A partner: someone who takes a vested interest in every aspect of your life including your professional success. You pool resources and opportunities. You include each other in decisions in all areas.

A provider: someone who takes on responsibilities of your unit, often financially. This person is the leader of the relationship and often funds the lifestyle of the couple.

Here's how each mate might respond when you come home from work with news to share.

"I got a promotion!"

WHAT A COMPANION MIGHT SAY

Congrats! Let me know how you want to celebrate.

WHAT A PARTNER MIGHT SAY

So proud of you! That strategy we talked about worked.

WHAT A PROVIDER MIGHT SAY

That's amazing! Will it require you to work more?

"I'm on deadline for a big project."

WHAT A COMPANION MIGHT SAY

Hope it goes well. Look forward to spending time together when you are done.

WHAT A PARTNER MIGHT SAY

I understand. Let me know if I can read over anything. I'll hold down home while you grind.

WHAT A PROVIDER MIGHT SAY

Rooting for you. I'm here if you need me.

"I just got laid off."

WHAT A COMPANION MIGHT SAY

Sorry to hear. I'll let you know if I hear of anything. Want to go out Saturday?

WHAT A PARTNER MIGHT SAY

That's their loss. We are going to be all right. We planned for surprises like this.

WHAT A PROVIDER MIGHT SAY

Sorry, baby. I got us. You can take a break from working if you like.

You can find happiness with a companion, partner, or a provider. Just be honest on what you desire and what type of relationship you are in. Many women have exhausted themselves trying to convert a companion into a partner. I realized as I grew professionally that I wanted a partner, someone who would take a vested interest in my success and someone who was open to me being a part of their success as well. My career is my life's work and not something I turn off when I go home. Three months into dating, Sir Brooklyn was on the set with me as I filmed a video with Netflix and gave me invaluable feedback. I could see he added value and was not intimidated by me or my career.

For Boss Brides, it's essential to date men who believe in you and your goals. I've been excited to see the number of men who want a woman who is passionate about her professional pursuits. Here are four signs a man will be an ally to your dreams:

How to Spot a Career-Supportive Guy

1. His Identity Isn't a Title
We all know those people who introduce themselves as "Jill from Jones Legal," or speak in plural when discussing their job ("We just bought a jet"). It's important to choose a guy who sees himself as an individual and not a walking résumé. People who are secure with themselves are able to be supportive of others because they don't see you as competition. When you mention your latest accomplishment at work, make sure your guy is able to be happy for you without needing to mention his own success.

2. He Sees a Goal Not Gender
Barbie now offers a building blocks set. The product isn't from a focus group of five-year-olds, but a response to the push for girls to gain math skills early on, not to mention the growing number of fathers who are doing toy shopping for the family and spending more time with their kids. Today, there is an increased sharing of household duties for

marriages and more than 40 percent of American homes have women who earn more money. When dating a guy, listen closely as he talks about the type of family and marriage he wants. Does he see washing dishes or going to a PTA meeting as "women's work"? Easily jump-start the conversation by asking, "Have you ever changed a diaper?" You may be surprised by the answer.

3. He's Farsighted

The most successful professionals understand delayed gratification. In choosing a partner, you want someone who will understand you may have to work late for a year to position yourself for a promotion that will give you more flexibility and increase your salary. While dating, take note if your guy is willing to deny immediate pleasures for a bigger goal. Is he eating less takeout to save toward a new car? Is he working over a three-day weekend to enjoy two weeks in China with his college friends? Someone who has experienced sacrifice will understand when your family needs to make tough short-term decisions to position yourself for a stronger future.

4. He Knows the Cast

As a Boss Bride, you are passionate about your career. That also means you regularly talk about the highs and lows of your current position to your social circle, including the man in your life. When seeing if a guy has long-term qualities, pay attention to how he engages with you when it comes to your career. Does he just ask about your day or does he check in on how your presentation went? Does he remember the backstory and your boss's name when you share the latest tale? You want a partner who pays attention to where you are and supports where you are going.

It takes an emotionally mature and secure man to have a healthy relationship with a powerful woman. Trying to placate an insecure man takes energy you can't afford. For most of us, that's more time and energy than we have. Stay focused up front if a man is comfortable with your growing success.

Working Wives Confessions: Dating as a Powerhouse

"After all of these years, I've realized we are unequally yoked when it comes to business and professional pursuits. I'm always on the path to success and he's okay with being sedentary and mediocre. I will work from sun up to sun down, and keep my lines of communication open with my husband. He will work all day and never check in or say hi."

"All the men I dated prior to my husband hated that I was always on the road and would fight me about it. My husband just gets it!"

"I'm a high-achieving, high-performing female entrepreneur. I know many women like me who get support from their significant others yet still feel nervous about growing too big or too far beyond their partners. I'd rather wake up every day knowing that I allowed my light, enthusiasm, and purpose guide my life, not fear of my partner's insecurity."

As a dating coach in my career and personal life, many women call on me to hook them up with a great guy. I have been a matchmaker for many women—from setting actress Yvette Nicole Brown up on her first blind date to hosting a dating boot camp with Steve Harvey for single teachers. Yes, getting support in your dating life is smart! I also remind women the best matchmaker in our life is our own self. Let's review your checklist to get you ready for your real-life Mr. Right. Let your heart's desires and love for yourself guide you in your quest, and not your ego. One of the reasons I stayed in a relationship that had expired is my ego liked the way he looked on my arm. I had to check myself and my criteria.

Check Your Checklist

HIS LOOKS

Asking "What's your type?" gets many women thinking about the genetic makeup of a man. The truth is, a perfect nose can't rub your feet at night and a six-pack won't remember your mother's birthday. When looking for a life partner, instead of just taking note of his outward presentation, pay attention to his true self.

After a string of breakups, Atlanta librarian Neely realized her focus on what her perfect man would look like had her minimizing what he should be like. "My dream guy was a man with a dark complexion and a head full of hair," she says. "My ex had everything physically I wanted. When he ended things, I looked at myself and realized I had not been tuned in to whether he was good to me." Her next boyfriend had fair skin and a bald head, yet offered her the love she craved. "Now I love the bald head, not any bald head, but his," she says. "I took the physical items off my list and allowed the right man to find me."

Focusing on a man's heart and not his packaging is something actress Niecy Nash preaches as Hollywood's dating guru. "Sometimes people confuse their preference with their priority," says the author and former host of *Let's Talk About Love*. "Preference is all the outer wrapping. What should be your priority are qualities of a lasting relationship."

HIS LIFESTYLE

When looking for love, it's important to recognize the difference between a man's circumstances and his characteristics. Circumstances—like being rich or broke—are things that can change. However, characteristics are qualities that last a lifetime. If the cutie you met doesn't take the time to open your door to his Mercedes, you may have a better experience with the gentleman in the Honda. "Be honest about what you really need and what's important to you," Nash says. "You have to have the mind-set, **I want what is best for me**."

Michelle Singletary, a nationally syndicated columnist for *The Wash-*

ington Post, was dating two men at the same time her toilet broke. One suitor told her to call a plumber, while the other offered to fix the problem. She committed to the guy who showed up with the tools. He also proposed to her with the two-third-carat engagement ring he could afford instead of the one-carat ring she desired. "I realized that he was the kind of man I wanted for a husband," she says. "He wasn't going to overspend. It was a value I respected." While dating, Singletary also asked questions to see what kind of family man he would be. "Even though we were in our twenties, I asked where he saw himself when he retired. He replied on the back porch watching his grandkids. We were compatible for the long term."

YOUR PATTERN

In fine-tuning your partner expectations, review your dating history for any subconscious checklist items you could lose. Have the last few guys you've dated been emotionally unavailable or perpetually between jobs? You may be unknowingly seeking a certain characteristic.

Sabrina, twenty-seven, realized her attraction to bad boys had led to three broken hearts. "I was looking for a certain swag, and that demeanor always came with a guy who was a jerk," she admits. Sabrina raised her standards to a man who treated her as a prize and protected her heart. Soon an old friend asked her out. When she'd first met him nine years earlier, his lack of style made her look right past him. Now she could see he was caring and that they shared many interests. "I was so shallow when we first met, and it blinded me to this man," she says. "He's more than I ever could have asked for."

Seek Your Complement—Not Your Clone

I often remind powerful women that you don't need another you. We think if we are super-busy and building a business then ideally our partner will too. While it's important you be compatible, you don't need a clone. You want someone to bring things to the table that you don't.

There is someone special for all of us, though he may not show up as expected. If you ever need a reminder, Google can tell you about a guy who owed thousands in student loans and had holes in his shoes when he met a woman named Michelle. His name is Barack Obama.

Your Checklist Cheat Sheet

Start with the following essential qualities in a partner.

1. CARING. Having a man who treats you right is nonnegotiable.

2. DRIVEN. When you're both dedicated to pursuing your personal passions while contributing to the relationship, it creates a dynamic you can build on together, something you need as a Boss Bride.

3. SENSE OF HUMOR. With all life's ups and downs, being able to laugh together and not take things or yourself too seriously is essential for a strong relationship.

4. HONEST. You need to be able to trust any man you're thinking of sharing your life with. If the new guy lies to his boss to hang with you, it's only a matter of time before you are on the receiving line of his deception.

Next add the following:

- List the experiences you want to have with your partner. Put your ego to the side and ask your heart what it wants and if you want support, visit www.myheartwants.com.

- List the core values and characteristics you are seeking.

- List how your partner will make you feel.

- Highlight the nonnegotiables you listed so you are focused on what matters most to you in a partner.

When I was unexpectedly single while beginning to write this book, I wrote a list titled "The Man I Will Marry." I included the experiences we would share and the qualities he would possess. What was most important to me was a man who knew God and prayed. Months later I met Sir Brooklyn. He was funny, smart, caring, cute, and thoughtful. What made me give him a real chance was our spiritual connection. The night before my birthday we both were sleepily talking on the phone and I wondered why we didn't just hang up. At 11:59 p.m. he said, "It's your birthday!" I smiled and thanked God for making it through another year with all its highs and lows. I thought about my breakup and my new beginning with the man on the other end of the phone.

At 12:00 a.m. on February 8, 2017, he sang me three versions of "Happy Birthday" (the traditional, the Stevie Wonder classic, and *The Simpsons* version with Michael Jackson). "I wanted to be the first person to wish you a happy birthday," he said. In my mid-swoon he started praying over me and thanking God for bringing me this far and claiming another amazing year. His prayer was my testimony of the importance of getting clear on what you really need in a partner. He's sexy and has many of my preferences, but leading with my priority helped me find what I actually needed.

I'll be the first to admit looks do matter. Your match should fulfill you in every way. We all want to be attracted to our partners and you need chemistry to have a passionate relationship. What I have learned after interviewing hundreds of couples and from my own life is that when you lead with seeking your core values, you set the foundation for a strong relationship. Then physical attraction is the cherry on top, and not the whole sundae. This also minimizes you being distracted by charming, attractive men who don't have substance and will block the type of person you deserve. And by leading with core values, many women have found themselves falling for people they may have looked right past if they were focused solely on the physical.

Having a checklist keeps you focused on what you really need and not just the flash. I always thought Carrie Bradshaw could do better than Mr. Big. Yes, he was successful, smooth, and handsome, but he was not trustworthy or honorable. And turns out the glamorized TV version isn't reality. In real life Candace Bushnell, who wrote *Sex and the City*, didn't end up with the real life Mr. Big. He dumped her and married someone else. Get clear on your priorities early to minimize the chance of heartache down the road.

Beware of Soul Diggers

Attention, powerful women: Beware of Soul Diggers. Men are raised with the messaging all around warning them of gold diggers, women who seek to use a man for financial support. Well, women aren't being told at the same levels to watch out for preying men. I have seen an alarming rise in women getting got by Soul Diggers, men who use them for emotional support without pouring any back in, leaving women depleted. With the higher rates of women making moves in their careers, while simultaneously being raised to be nurturing, we are perfectly primed to be preyed on by men who we think need a little TLC. These Soul Diggers end up draining women of not only resources, but time and energy that they can never get back. It is not your job to raise a grown man. If his potential hasn't converted to results, it is not your job to close the gap. Being centered around what you are seeking helps to minimize the chances of you being with someone who does not have what it takes for the long haul. And by opening up your dating pool, which we will cover in this chapter, you will increase your exposure to compatible partners and minimize the chance of you settling for a Soul Digger.

After getting clear on what you want it's time to officially open your heart and schedule to love. But first let's be clear on what exactly a date is since we missed out on the era of courting.

Define a "Date"

I was looking over the menu and glanced up to see him looking at me. In that second it dawned on me that the friend I thought I was catching up with thought he was on a date. With our increasingly "it's complicated" dating world, knowing if you are or aren't on a date has become a blurred line. Sixty-nine percent of singles are confused by what makes a date, according to *USA Today*.

And as a Boss Bride we have to be especially clear, since we are often prone to meet people in networking scenarios and be invited to talk work projects, increasing the chance of confusion.

So what exactly makes an outing a date?

The biggest difference in hanging out and an actual date is the intention. That's it! You can have a five-course dinner that isn't a date. Or sit in the park just talking and it *is* a date.

What separates a date isn't the location or the length of the encounter. What makes a date is the clear understanding of both parties that they are exploring the possibility of a romantic involvement.

The reason we end up asking ourselves *Is this a date?* while cheesecake is served is because we haven't gotten clear on both parties' expectations. To minimize your chances of dating confusion, get the uncomfortable part out of the way before the could-be date. Use a lighthearted tone and your bright smile to ask your requestor, "Why do you want to go out?" This answer will frame the outing and leave you from feeling unsure.

Otherwise you may find yourself smizing over a cocktail sitting across from your crush. You're elated your secret snuggle fantasy has finally asked you out. He leans over with fresh breath and whispers in your ear to ask if your best friend is interested in him. He figured you would know and could save him the awkwardness if she's not.

Getting clear beforehand may save you a lot of time and confusion. A few years back, I found myself on a series of what I called sneak-attack dates. They were with men I thought were professional colleagues who asked me to meet up for a drink or dinner. They had never been flirtatious toward me so I thought the outings were strictly platonic. Then once we were out I could tell their intention was for a date. Now I see clearly how silly my thinking was. Single men rarely ask single women out to dinner or drinks as strictly friends or to talk business. Even if they haven't officially asked you out on a date, most single guys are open to the possibility of dating a woman they invite out somewhere. So Boss Brides, always be clear before you head out.

Define Your Love Goals

Many times we compromise on the type of person we date because we believe the great guy we desire is not within our reach. I am here as a living witness of hundreds of couples, eligible bachelors, and my own life that great love is within the reach of anyone courageous enough to expect it and reach. This quote by my writer shero and legendary playwright Lorraine Hansberry has been seared on my soul since college: **"A woman who is willing to be herself and pursue her own potential runs not so much the risk of loneliness, as the challenge of exposure to more interesting men—and people in general."**

It was my comfort that it was okay to go full out for my career and men wouldn't be intimidated by my ambition. It was my motivation to put energy into meeting the incredible and interesting men she talks about when I settled into New York City. I have met many women who have met their great love by dipping into the international single sea. There's Aja in Atlanta who met her husband during a relocation to Australia and brought him back with her. And my old manager Sharon met her husband, Darren, by opening her Match.com profile to meet men around the world. He moved from the United Kingdom to New Jersey when they wed.

In my coaching practice, I see much higher success from clients who commit to measurable outcomes for their goals. I also saw the same for myself. My defined goal of two dates in a month in 2008 gave me a confidence boost and real pressure to explore new ways to meet people and even to make the first move because I had a concrete benchmark to hit.

Get in the habit of setting measurable goals in every area of life.

Save the Date: Set a Dating Goal

Commit to a definitive goal in your love life for this month and do a crazy eight of ways you can get to your goal. Ask a friend to be your accountability partner and put it on your calendar to celebrate as if it's already done: "I went on three dates this month. You can call me Cupid."

Love Goal: Work Your Flirt

One of the reasons I was able to go on plenty of dates and meet new people all the time is my strong flirt muscle. I'm stereotypically southern so smiling and talking to strangers is natural. But being a great flirt isn't just nature, it can be a nurtured and learned skill. First, remember flirting is simply showing interest in someone, whether romantic or not. It does not have to feel forced or intense. Your flirting should be natural to your personality and style. Here's how you can strengthen your flirt muscle in meeting new people.

Be an equal opportunity flirt. The more you practice flirting, the better you become at using your charm when you need it most, like when that cute guy steps onto the elevator. Before you walk out the door decide you will be your best, which brings out the best in others. Your smile can be contagious. Flex your flirt muscles daily by complimenting the delivery guy on his watch or asking your neighbor on the train what he's reading.

Let your body talk. Most men have been rejected when approaching women, which can make them gun-shy. Signaling your interest reassures a man he has a chance. Smile, make eye contact, and don't be afraid to get a little physical. Pat a man on the tie as you compliment the color. Sir Brooklyn likes to remind me I touched his beard the night we met.

Sit pretty. Location matters when working a room. Next time you're at happy hour, sit at a high table or at the bar instead of a booth or corner nook. Be near the action and where you can see and be seen.

Work the room. Don't limit your attention to the guy who catches your eye. You build your social currency when you talk to people you don't know. Chatting up the bartender or the lady at the next table signals to the rest of the room that you are friendly and fun.

Embracing your inner flirt also can help your finances. A recent University of California, Berkeley, study found that flirting was beneficial for women in negotiating and even could help women get a lower cost on a car. "Women are uniquely confronted with a trade-off in terms of being perceived as strong versus warm. Using feminine charm in negotiation is a technique that combines both," says Laura Kray, study author and professor. Whether protecting your pockets or meeting your future fiancé, the art of flirting is a skill that comes from not taking yourself too seriously and enjoying the journey. Commit to unleash your mojo.

Love Goal: Date More

For busy women one of the biggest complaints I hear is "Where are the men?" and "I'm too busy to meet anybody." As a Boss Bride, you can make the most of your resources and realize every day is a new day to meet someone amazing. Slow down and enjoy every second of your life—which is a great way to notice more amazing people in your path. In my quest for a year of hot dates I had a wide range of suitors—friends setting me up on blind dates, male friends fighting to get out of the friend zone, and new men I met online, on Facebook, or while out and about.

Hang Where He Hangs

Now that you have refined what you are looking for in a partner, bring your checklist to life. How would he spend his days? It will help you keep in mind his lifestyle and how you would be compatible. Having a clear picture of the type of person you hope to date is critical. One client showed me the glaring mistake many professional single women make.

She was a fabulous jet-setter in the fashion industry yet was down about her dating life. I had her describe her day and also her ideal guy and the experiences she wanted to have with him. She spent most of her days at fashion events and traveling, yet yearned for an Aidan: Carrie's laid-back, carpenter boyfriend on *Sex and the City*. She fantasized about them remodeling a home together. Her professional pursuits had taken over her life and she was not meeting handymen at the DVF sample sale. We set up a strategy to engage with more guys who fit her ideal that included going to home improvement workshops and yard sales with friends to cultivate her own knowledge for her dreams and be in places with the type of guy she desired.

Spread the Word

The majority of married couples today still meet through their social circles of church, school, work, community organizations, family, and friends. The same way you send out your résumé to trusted contacts when looking for jobs, share with your network that you are looking to connect with interesting people. And when you bump into an old friend asking how you are doing, mention you are on a date challenge looking to connect with cool people and to send any your way. You can totally blame me and say that this book pushed you to do it.

Try a Blind Date

For women looking to quickly get back in the swing of dating, try the adventure of a blind date. "My date was a guy I would have walked right past on the street," says Detroit dater Nina, who met her blind date through OKCupid's now defunct Crazy Blind Date feature. "It was a great experience and forced me out of my comfort zone." Let the outgoing and connected people in your life know you want to knock a blind date off your bucket list. Meeting and dating guys you would never marry is a great thing. And yes some toads may slip in. Meeting different guys helps you refine your checklist of items that are essential in your mate and those things you can live without.

The Ring: Spot Dating Success
Hit up a friend who has no problems meeting people. Set a date to hit the streets. It's a double win as you catch up with a friend and strengthen your own flirt muscle. If you are in New York City and I'm free, let's go.

Look Online

More than 30 percent of couples marrying now meet online. We use the internet for buying bridesmaids gowns, paying bills, and finding a place to live, so why not log on for a Friday night date? "Like anything else in life, what you choose to prioritize gets done. You are not going to get in great physical shape without going to the gym. In the same way, you are not going to just meet someone great without being active," Sam Yagan, vice chair of Match.com and cofounder of OKCupid, told me.

We use technology for everything else and it can be a great resource for successful singles. My recommended online dating strategy for Boss Brides is to diversify your profiles by signing up for at least two sites, including a large site and a niche site based on your interests or demographic.

When it comes to selecting sites, you often get what you pay for, so if you are in the market for something more serious instead of just the fun of dating, I suggest investing in a paid account like Match to increase your chances of a quality guy also looking for something serious.

LARGE DATING SITES/APPS

Match

Tinder

Bumble

Coffee Meets Bagel

OKCupid

eHarmony

The Inner Circle

Hinge

PlentyOfFish

Zoosk

NICHE SITES
ChristianMingle
BlackPeopleMeet
JDate
Meld
It's Just Lunch

Boss Bride Online Dating Cheat Sheet

1. Open your heart and account. I understand signing up for an online dating website might be a lot for some Boss Brides, especially if you are publicly known thanks to your hot career. I still encourage you to view it as a tool to meet people and not a symbol of your single status. And remember even Martha Stewart and MC Lyte signed up for Match.com, and Lyte met her husband on the site. Tatyana Ali grew from portraying Ashley Banks on *The Fresh Prince of Bel-Air* to meeting her husband on eHarmony. So yes, there are high-profile women (and men) online. And yes, there may be some weirdos on all these sites, just like there are in real life. Stay focused on expanding your pool and embrace the experience. One of the best things about being single again last year was I got to finally make my own Bumble profile instead of living through my clients and friends. I reconnected with a guy I used to work with and he was the first guy to bake for me. And just by having a profile I got a smooth dinner invite in my Instagram DMs from a cutie who saw my profile and got proactive. Online dating is about expanding your single sea and increasing your chances of meeting a compatible partner.

2. Make your profile pop. A dating profile is not a résumé. Instead of trying to fit all of your amazingness in witty phrases, focus on showing off a few specific parts of your personality. Share what you like to do for fun so the single on the other side can easily imagine what a date with you might entail. Instead of stating that you like new experiences share how much fun you had learning to make pasta in Italy or attending an astronomy lecture (I really highlighted these in my profile). Also be clear of your end goal rather than just saying you're looking for a casual relationship or "open to someone special."

3. Be an online flirt. If you still aren't ready for a dating profile, you can use other social networks to make friends and flirt. If you meet someone while out, connect with him on LinkedIn, Facebook, or Twitter and engage. I also challenge you to use Facebook's graph search to discover friends of friends with similar interests. You can easily discover people with similar interests in your network and can be as specific as you want with searches like "Single friends of my friends who live in Chicago and are between thirty and forty years old and who like *Game of Thrones* and Kendrick Lamar's music." Commit to reaching out to one likeminded person a month.

4. Date IRL. Online dating is a misnomer. It's really online meeting to potentially date in the real world. After you message for a little and you feel comfortable, things should graduate to phone calls and then a casual meet-up in person (a thirty-minute coffee is plenty) to assess real-world connection and chemistry. You should not be messaging anyone for more than a month in the same city without meeting.

5. Check your choices. Digital dating is a great opportunity to see your tastes in real time. Being on Tinder did not disappoint in the drama. The first guy I matched with had this really progressive profile. It wasn't until he messaged with witty banter before inquiring about hooking up, that I realized he was a guy I'd met before—because he lived in my building. Eek. But it wasn't all bad. I got the gift of seeing up close who I gravitated to with the dozens of matches and what they had in common.

Boss Bride Cutie Hot Spots

During my year of becoming a professional dater, by far my favorite hot spot for meeting men was the airport. The anticipation of traveling gave me a confidence boost to get my flirt on.

That spring I had a Friday night flight to my hometown of Atlanta. At the gate I spotted a cute guy. Once we started boarding, I noticed he was sitting near where my seat was to be. I walked back wondering if I would have the pleasure of sitting next to him for the flight. Finally I made it to 18D. He was in the seat right behind me. Almost. We made some serious eye contact and said hello, then settled into our seats. When I landed, I was so excited to get home, I didn't look back when exiting. Two days later I am at the airport waiting on my return flight and who do I spot? The same cutie I flew down with at the gate. We board the same flight again and this time we are sitting far apart. I smile at him as I take my seat at the front.

Back in New York, I exit the plane and take my time heading to baggage claim. After grabbing my bag, I feel a tap on my shoulder. I turn and there he is, smiling. "So you were on my plane going down and coming back?" I nod yes. He asks if I am visiting New York or returning. I say I am based in New York and he physically exhales. Three days later we have our first date, which leads to a two-month affair before he moved back to London. Here are a few other hot spots for Boss Brides to meet eligible bachelors.

HOTEL BARS

The best hotels in town and places that host large conferences are a traveler's oasis and perfect locations to meet interesting personalities.

Opening line: "So I take it you aren't here for the clown convention?"

COFFEE SHOPS

Find a table and spot the solo visitors. A friendly face is always welcomed while working or reading.

Opening line: "I'm heading up. Would you like a refill?" or "I'm finished with the paper. Great piece on _____."

CONFERENCES

Mix business and pleasure with professional conferences. Most have mixers for attendees, which is the perfect opportunity to expand your network and discover who has dating potential.

Opening line: "Is this your first time attending?"

TRAVEL HUBS

Make the most of layovers and flight delays with a large pool of power players and jet-setters. Hit up bars, lounges, and those charging corners with everyone huddled around the outlets.

Opening line: "Where are you headed?"

GYM

Get fit while being flirty. Use the many mirrors to make eye contact and recognize every guy wants to show he is athletic.

Opening line: "Can you spot me?"

ALUMNI EVENTS

Use the communality to strike up conversations with cute strangers. Ride the nostalgia to a nightcap.

Opening line: "Did you live in the [insert name of popular dorm]?"

COMMUNITY AND CHARITY EVENTS

We are the world. Get two for one by helping the planet while expanding your dating pool with positivity. Check out local nonprofits, churches, political action groups, and philanthropic efforts.

Opening line: "I love this organization. How did you get involved?"

MEET-UPS AND NETWORKING EVENTS

We still often date people who are a lot like us. Increase your chances of meeting likeminded men by joining different meet-ups and Facebook groups. Tech and start-up groups on meetup.com often overindex in smart men.

Opening line: "What's your favorite app?"

Remember you have nothing to lose from starting the conversation. "I met my wife and she was the first woman to ever approach me. It's nice to do something different that no one else has done for your guy," shared Darryl, a husband of one of the Working Wives.

Secrets of Successful Daters

One of my favorite stories I ever worked on was heading to the front lines of dating and getting the best advice from those who see couples on dates regularly—waitresses, hairstylists, and couples out on dates. Here are some of the top tips I discovered.

Get Ready for Your Date

- Road test new outfits before wearing them on a date. You will know what kind of undergarments work best and be more confident on your date.

- Give yourself enough time to prepare for a date. Instead of talking to a girlfriend while getting dressed, burn candles and play music to set the mood.

- Embrace your femininity with a flattering dress and avoid heavy makeup. Try red, pink, green, or blue. Your look is a reflection of your personality.

Build Something Solid

- Get to his house and look at his surroundings. How he lives will tell you what's important to him. How his pets act is a reflection of his behavior.

- A DC florist shared that a lot of guys are so nervous ordering flowers for you. Don't be afraid to express yourself, because he probably is feeling it inside. Guys can be shy.

- Do exactly what you say you're going to do. If you're not going to be able to make it, give a person a call. If you're not feeling this person, be up-front and honest.

How a Few Boss Brides Found Love

Road Test: "He showed up five minutes before the cutoff in yellow pants, yellow shoes, and drove an orange Pinto with a 'for sale' sign in the back," Constance says of her husband, Vincent. They still had a great time. And turns out the clothes and car were just a test to see if she was dating the man or the BMW and big house he owned. They've been married for twenty-five years.

Flying Solo: Carla was a Los Angeles–based workaholic, clocking sixty hours a week as a celebrity assistant. To unwind, she and her friends planned a girls' getaway to Florida. Right before the trip, all three friends canceled, so she went alone. Because of her upbeat attitude about the situation a friend in Miami set her up on a blind date with Jason. "I just planned to relax on the beach," she says. "Little did I know, I would meet the love of my life." On their first date, the couple danced till 7:00 a.m. at a reggae club. "She was so easy-going," Jason remembers.

Open Position: After meeting at a mutual friend's baby shower, Mack and Sasha became Skype buddies. A month into their conversations, Sasha sent a written application to Mack to be her boyfriend, which he completed and passed. "I knew only someone serious would complete it," she says. "A man doesn't have to be perfect—just perfect for you."

Giving your suitor an application is brilliant and very Boss Bride! Being as intentional in our personal lives as we are in our careers is essential. We also have to examine what hasn't worked in our past to bring those lessons into the present.

I've only gone back to a man once. After a long day at work, I went to the Caribbean restaurant around the corner from my Harlem apartment to escape from the publishing industry into stewed chicken, cabbage, and ginger beer.

Walking home I passed two men. I was too busy replaying the day to pay them close attention. Once I walked past a male voice said, "Hey beautiful. How are you?" This was pet peeve number 378 about men. Why wait until I have passed by to say something? I kept going.

"Come back . . . I'm cute," he said with a smile in his voice. Curiosity killed this cat. I turned around to see if he was lying. He was not.

I walked back and he introduced himself. He was tall. Really tall. I gave him my number (I was in the midst of my year of dating) and went on my way to dive into my dinner. The next day he called. He was at the gym. Turns out he was an NBA player.

We went on a magical first date with candlelight and went out a few more times before he dropped off the planet—or so it seemed. Turns out he wasn't still an NBA player when we met and he had just been cut. He had moved across the globe to play in another country. And, oh yeah, was engaged to be married and had a young daughter. I found this all out after the fact from Google. I hadn't wanted to feel like a stalker so I didn't check him out closely online when we first met, only confirming he was a professional player in the NBA without looking to see that he had been cut right before we met. The idea of an unexpected romance with someone "super-successful" prevented me from exhausting every resource to protect myself. So absolutely do a thorough search on a potential suitor for red flags and do not accidentally like a picture from a year ago.

The only time you shouldn't google a guy is if it's Morris Chestnut and you are about to interview him. Do not. I repeat. DO NOT GOOGLE HIM. It seems innocent enough to want to make sure you have your facts straight. But what you may forget is that he had an eight-pack and is shirtless in low-slung sweats in a scene in *The Best Man Holiday*. And that image will pop right up as you diligently try to be a professional.

And then he will be in your ear laughing at your lame jokes and you will be staring at his eight-pack in front of you. And then you would ask your questions and fight to ignore how he really is smart and thoughtful and charming. A lethal combination if you fell in love with Lance Sullivan over a decade before and realize that the man who plays him is even better. And then you might have to go tell a coworker you've been charmed. And find yourself actually lying on her office floor. Not that this happened to me. I just imagine this could happen. So again. Say it with me. DON'T GOOGLE MORRIS CHESTNUT.

When I interviewed him I had to ask what about his wife made him realize he could see a future for them.

His response:

I have been with my wife for a number of years now and the number one thing that keeps us strong is a mutual respect; that is first and foremost. I like to think of myself as pretty perceptive. I am always watching and listening more than I am talking. And when I met my wife, there were a lot of qualities I was paying attention to. I knew that she would be a great mother just from how she cared for her nephew and her family. She respected her mother and she respected her family. Those were some of the qualities that I saw that I thought would make her a great partner.

And what is one thing that we as women might be surprised to know about men?

What would be important is for women to understand that men don't have it all figured out. There are so many different dynamics to a woman and so many different things that women in general go through that men just don't understand. I like to call it beautifully complex. Unless a woman is involved with a straight knucklehead, sometimes you just need to be a little bit more patient with a man or a potential partner because he may not be as perceptive or he may not be as informed as it seems.

Thanks, Morris. We will keep that in mind.

We spend so much time on our smart phones and not just for online searching potential suitors. We have to talk about how your phone can impact your entire life and career.

Let's Talk About Sext

In 2014 security software company McAfee released the report, "Love, Relationships & Technology." The research found that 54 percent of US adults use their mobile devices to send or receive sexual content through texts, emails, videos, or photos. Forty-five percent of those adults save the content. That's right: more than half of us sext and almost half of the content is saved.

Terry, thirty-two, wasn't thinking about any of that when she met a guy online in 2008 and sent him topless photos two weeks later, she shared with *Essence*. They went out a few times, but didn't progress. They faded out amicably, or so Terry thought. About a year later, she got a call from the human resources department at her engineering job. "I had found a new job and was relocating," she says. "I thought they were calling for an exit interview."

Instead, the HR director asked Terry if someone had a vendetta against her since the entire leadership team at the company had received an email containing topless photos of her. "I immediately started crying," she recalls, as I'm sure many of us would too. "My job assured me they would investigate and that even if I wasn't leaving the company, they wouldn't have fired me. My managers had seen me topless and it was hard to look my boss in the eye."

We can learn from Terry's misfortune.

#BossBride Vow

- I vow to never send nude pics to folks who haven't earned that right.
- I vow to keep my face out of my sexy pics if I do decide to sext someone I completely trust and to always argue it wasn't me if they surface.

Label Your Love

Imagine you've been doing the work of an executive vice president, building an entire company, being there late nights, and creating infrastructure. At the company party the CEO introduces you as the intern. That's what happens when we pour into relationships without the proper boundaries and titles.

Mislabeling in matters of the heart is mighty dangerous. Don't do the work if you don't get the perks and title. Don't give commitment when you aren't sure you are receiving it in return.

As Boss Bride Bill of Rights number 6 says, "I have the right to create boundaries in every area of my life and to teach people how to treat me."

Instead of the "What are we?" question, which gives the power to the other person, state your desires plainly and ask the other person where they stand. "I am in the market for something committed that can turn long term. Let me know what you are looking for." It's also important to state up front your desires to avoid falling for someone whose choices don't align with yours.

Our time is too precious to assume how the other person feels. Always be up front on your desires and listen closely to where someone you are dating stands. With my coaching clients, having the awkward conversations is something we practice so they can quickly get clarity in any scenario by asking the right questions. Clarity in every area of your life leads to wholeness and happiness. So get to asking before you head out that door.

And just as a friend with benefits isn't a boyfriend, a boyfriend isn't a husband. Once you settle into a relationship continue to make clear your desires and expectations. Discuss your ideal timeline of how long you look to date before exploring marriage and discuss a framework that works for you both. Decide for yourself the experiences that are only for your husband.

#BossBride Vow

- I vow to always get clarity in my relationships. If commitment is what I seek, I will wait to have what I desire before sharing my body, spirit, and space prematurely.

Dating to Relationship

If you were interviewing for a job, and had not been offered the position, would you go on other interviews? Your answer better be "Absolutely!"

As a Boss Bride, it is completely fine to date multiple guys at the same time, as long as you aren't sexually involved with any. I recommend waiting until after a commitment if you are in the market for something serious.

Dating multiple guys gives you the chance to assess qualities and get clearer on what your needs are, as Michelle Singletary found out earlier in this chapter when her toilet broke.

Stay open and honest with all guys that you are seeing other people. This often makes men realize they don't have the option to string you along and if they are truly interested (and they are if they're smart and mature enough to see you are a prize) they will step up and formalize a commitment.

I encourage you to examine suitors closely. Who sleeps in your bed and lives in your heart is the most important decision you will make. Take your time. It's much easier to promote people who have earned their way to your inner circle than to try to ease someone out who was not properly vetted.

I've found there are Four Cs for dating just like there are for diamonds.

Four Cs for a Powerful Partnership

1. **Circumstances:** What are our current situations and lifestyles?

2. **Characteristics:** What are our innate qualities and personality traits? How do you both adapt to change and when you disagree?

3. **Compatibility:** Are our values and lives in alignment?

4. **Chemistry:** Is there a spark and connection for us to build on?

When dating, review the Four Cs to assess if you are in alignment. A lasting relationship needs all Four Cs for its best shot at succeeding. It's important to be with someone who can effectively course correct when things don't go as planned and that you can do the same.

Unfortunately, our society looks mostly at circumstances for making lifelong decisions like marriage, when this C is the most fragile and likely to change. Circumstances include fine and rich. All things that can change in an instant, while characteristics are innate traits such as being caring, strategic, and resourceful, which will last a lifetime. A lot of chemistry can sometimes mask if there is true compatibility. Having hot Saturday nights together is not enough if it doesn't lead to comparable plans on Sunday.

One of my favorite songs is "A Sunday Kind of Love" by Etta James. I had never been so happy to wash dishes in my life the first time I heard it. I was grinning and busting suds inside the home of legendary *Essence* editor Susan L. Taylor, learning what the lyrics truly meant.

It was 2006 and she spoke that day to the summer interns at the magazine. After an empowering talk, she invited a few of us to her place that evening for an informal cocktail party she was hosting. Three of us took her up on the offer and headed uptown. We entered a stunning skyscraper close to the West Side Highway with a gorgeous view of the Hudson. We didn't have to tell the front desk who we were going to see before he directed us to go to level three. We got in the elevator and didn't see a "3." Then it clicked. He was saying "PH3." As in "penthouse."

We walked in and the room was filled with emotion and energy. As Susan and her husband shared a chair and unconsciously grazed each other's arms, women around the room talked culture and politics. Just as quickly as things began, the evening wrapped up. The room of influential women thinned.

Susan drafted us to help close out the party and we were elated. As I started the water for dishes, she began to offer more wisdom on life and love. She shared how the penthouse had been a dream of hers to have a place to share with people, just as she had done that night. The view was gorgeous as we looked out at the Hudson River and the sunset. Then her husband came into the room and you could feel the electricity between these two after years together. She always tells women to talk to your man with love, about the difference your tone and adding a "baby" or "honey" can make. And she practiced what she preached as she sweetly asked him to put on Etta James.

"A Sunday Kind of Love" came on the speakers and it was like the soundtrack to the moment, as the two hugged up and talked about their love for Etta. This powerful woman knew how to be a partner. Dishes done, I mentioned my sore throat and she made me ginger tea and gave me some ginger for the road.

I was enjoying the New York dating scene. But seeing her in that kitchen as Etta sang made me want what they were drinking. I never used the rest of the ginger. But "A Sunday Kind of Love" has stayed with me.

The good news is this is the best time in history to be an ambitious woman ready for love. As I sat on a date with a cute six-foot-two Swedish humanitarian who works at the United Nations and plays the saxophone, I thought this is the perk no one tells professional women about. To be amazing is to meet more amazing people.

A few years ago my cousin Tia got married. She and her Mr. Right met on MySpace, back when it was cool to be on MySpace. At the reception the DJ played Beyoncé's "Single Ladies," the official bouquet toss anthem. I sashayed to the dance floor in my burgundy satin "you'll wear it again" bridesmaid dress. Among the sea of unmarried women, I positioned myself perfectly when I spotted a new competitor joining the fray: my mother, a divorcée in her sixties ready to try again at love. I could only laugh as we both leaped for a sign that a fulfilling marriage was still within our reach.

The dating landscape has definitely shifted for women. It is also all our own. Commit to playing an active role in creating the relationship of your dreams.

Whispers of a Woman

WHAT EACH WORKING WIFE WOULD SAY TO HERSELF AS SHE WALKED DOWN THE AISLE

The love you need is out there and available, start by looking in the mirror. Don't get wrapped up in money. Love, live, and enjoy the company of your mate. Stay focused on your love as opposed to the business. The latter will work itself out. **You can have it all.** Give lots of grace. You will let each other down, disappoint one another, sin against one another. Be quick to show grace and mercy and be forgiving. Always remember that the other person loves you and does not WANT to hurt you. Bad days happen, give them space. Hold them accountable for their actions, but be forgiving and remember that you too are a sinner in need of grace. **Remember you are a Queen.** Never take the love you have for granted. It is what will get you through it all. **WAIT. Be patient. You don't have to rush! God wants you to have the desires of your heart. They don't have to be in a specific order. All will come in due season.** Be flexible and let life happen. God has a plan, just ride along. **It is harder than it looks.** Be patient and forgiving. You aren't perfect, don't expect your partner to be.

Welcome to the Half-Time Party!

You are officially halfway through this book. *Congrats!*

We are conditioned to wait until we cross the finish line to celebrate life's milestones.

Well, as a Boss Bride, we live for the experience and pop champagne along the journey!

I salute you on making it to this page and congrats on every goal in your life that you are 27 percent, 41 percent, or 88 percent through. As a busy woman it's tempting to go from one accomplishment to the next chasing your ever-moving finish line. In constantly looking to the future, we can miss the magic of the moment and all we have achieved thus far.

Every step counts and deserves acknowledgment!

Here's your Boss Bride cheat sheet to add admiration to your regular routine.

1. Stay Toast Ready
The next time you are grocery shopping buy a bottle or two of bubbly. And when you have a kick-ass day or good news come your way, pop it

open. Life is a gift we unpack each day. Take every opportunity to clap and raise a glass.

2. Mark Your Movement
Each January and June I take inventory of what I've achieved and now I've started to celebrate each month. In my journal I list "Goals I achieved personally and professionally through focused effort" followed by "Goals I helped others achieve." Next I list moments and experiences that didn't have to happen for myself and others, from a clean bill of health to reconnecting with old friends.

3. Salute the Small Things
Did you find a way to give tough feedback in an effective way? Took the stairs at work? Wiped your makeup off before bed? Recognize the amazing little things you get done on a daily basis and give yourself the credit you deserve. You are pretty amazing.

4. Book Your Birthday
Whether you are turning thirty-four or forty-eight, it's a year you've never seen and an occasion worth celebrating. Send a save the date now to commemorate the miracle of doing an exciting activity with people you love. As I type, there is a suitcase open as I prepare to go to Antigua with my mom to celebrate our birthdays.

5. Look How Far You've Come
You may not be where you want to be just yet, but baby, you are not where you used to be. This year marks ten years since I graduated from college. And here I am owning my inner Boss Bride and sharing the journey with you. I am forever grateful. Connect with the woman you once were. She would be proud of you now.

4

GO HARD *AND* GO HOME

The more fearless we are in our personal lives, the more of that spirit we'll bring to changing our world.
—ARIANNA HUFFINGTON

It's finally here. My dream wedding has arrived, a special and intense time for a Boss Bride. I had been planning and prepping for this day for months, hoping every detail is perfect. I get up early at the Ritz-Carlton in Atlanta and take a bath to start this memorable day.

An old railroad station has transformed into a rustic venue for the ceremony and reception. Chandeliers hang over the dance floor, splashing light on exposed brick. A full candy bar with all my favorite sweets from cotton candy to Pop Rocks awaits the guests. The legendary Diann Valentine is the wedding designer and used her creativity to bring to life a magical wonderland in the middle of Atlanta, my hometown. Fuchsia lights alongside flickering candles make us feel in a faraway land. The tables are set to dine on roses, literally, with clear glass over stunning floral designs for us to feast on.

The R&B singer my high school self thought I would one day marry and whose picture was taped on my bedroom wall growing up is singing for my first dance as husband and wife. The day is perfect. I feel tears coming.

Teardrops of sadness sit inside my eyes. I realize I have planned my dream wedding for another couple.

Like many working women, I had put more energy into my job than into making my own dreams come true. As the editor for the *Essence* Storybook Wedding contest, I had produced this magical moment. Months before I sifted through hundreds of applications of men and women wanting to pop the question to their significant other. I narrowed it down to the best stories and our team settled on six finalists, who were flown to Walt Disney World to surprise their special someone with an enchanted proposal. Yes, girl. A surprise proposal at the happiest place on earth. I worked with each guy on the story to get his future fiancée to Disney (such as, "we won a radio contest for a free trip") and explain the presence of cameras on their nice excursion ("they want to capture our trip to share in marketing materials").

I helped produce every moment and watched as each man dropped to one knee. We had a proposal on a beach with rose petals sprinkled to say "Will You Marry Me?" One woman said "yes" at Animal Kingdom with giraffes and zebras looking on, while another man offered a lifetime of love after dancing at an outdoor café in Epcot with the Eiffel Tower overlooking them. And then there was the horse-and-buggy ride through a meadow before another man proposed.

Each moment was beautiful. The couple who received the most votes online for their love story and proposal would win a wedding package I was to manage. I booked the venue, called Diann, and was startled to realize my dream wedding wasn't my own. "Will my wedding be this nice?" I whispered to my best friend sitting next to me at the reception.

The groom was our friend Aaron from high school and he and his now wife, Kyla, won the contest. Their story of being college sweethearts followed by a long-distance romance when she moved for a job after graduation caught our team's attention. Their proposal at Victoria &

Albert's fine dining restaurant included a harpist playing "A Whole New World" as they had dessert. And after the surprise proposal, Kyla put her marketing skills to use to get votes for the Storybook Wedding prize package by getting the couple on Atlanta's V-103, the largest radio station in the South. Boss Bride indeed.

Their happiness was my wake-up call to get off the sidelines of my long-term personal goals. Unlike the newlyweds, it would probably be up to me and my partner to plan our wedding—and our lives.

We are a generation of women who have had the most professional opportunities of any before us. We are officially in "Boss" culture. We are asked to be a Girl Boss, Boss Bitch, and Boss Babes all while leaning in.

And with all that hustle it's important that we not only go hard in our professions, but also go home. We can maximize our potential while holding on to our innate femininity. We can find our equilibrium in pouring out into the world while pouring into ourselves.

Boss Bride Bill of Rights

2. I have the right to prioritize my personal life without sacrificing success. Who I spend my personal time with is just as important as my career. I can go hard *AND* go home.

No matter how amazing your position is, you cannot afford to marry your job. I have seen women across industries give their all to a company they don't own only to be shown the door unceremoniously.

And like a man, sometimes the more you keep your own identity and show you have options and are a hot commodity, the more your company appreciates and sees your value.

It's so tempting to give all of ourselves to work. To get addicted to the adrenaline of achievement. I'm writing to you on my lunch break while looking at the World Trade Center memorial. I am reminded how precious life is and how everyone who lost their lives on

September 11, 2001, wouldn't want another day in the office but would want more time with the people they loved most.

Live, girl, *live*.

And living starts with going full out in our life's purpose.

Go HARD

"I was sitting at my desk this morning thinking, I need something good to happen to me today. I thought I peaked when I hadn't run into my boss until 1:30 p.m. and then we had this awkward silence in the elevator because we secretly (well not so secret on my part) hate each other."

I laughed as one of my mentors sent me this message. And then I got really sad. If the best thing that happens during your day is to not see a boss you hate, well, that's not an awesome day.

You are the CEO of your life. And if anything isn't working—a crazy boss, an expired relationship, an exhausting commute—it's up to you to change it.

And that requires Going HARD. Going HARD doesn't mean working with your head down and giving your all to your work.

For a Boss Bride, Going HARD has a specific recipe.

HARD = **H**eart **A**ctions and **R**esearched **D**ecisions

Our life is built from the decisions we make each day.

Going HARD as a Boss Bride means making informed choices that give you life and looking inside first, then out. It is connecting with yourself and your purpose, then taking actions from your heart, not your ego.

Everything in life is a decision. And every decision leads to bigger decisions. Whether you get up early for work and ask for the raise gives you the option of where to go for a fabulous vacation. Whether you invest in yourself creates the option of others investing in you.

Even when we choose not to choose (as we say in Momentum Education), you are still making a decision.

POP QUIZ: AM I GOING HARD?

Ask yourself the following questions to see if you really are Going HARD.

- Have I written down my dreams and do I have a plan to achieve them?
- Am I making daily decisions that add to my life and move me toward my goals?
- Have I spoken with someone who has achieved what I hope to accomplish?

If the answer for all three questions isn't a loud YES, you can go harder.

I've heard many stories from women who are working hard and feel like they are getting nowhere. Often that's because they have not gotten a clear strategy on their goals and aligned with decision makers and stakeholders to support them. Before you can effectively and efficiently Go HARD, you have to get clear on where you are now and where you are going.

Going HARD at Work Baseline Checklist

❑ I know the core responsibilities of my current position and how what I do connects to the bottom line and the money my work generates or saves.

❑ I know the going rate for my skill level and position. I know how people with my same passions and talents make money.

❑ I completely understand my current compensation package and maximize the benefits offered to me by my employer.

❑ I have met with my manager to get a clear understanding of expectations and to share my goals for growth.

❑   I have met with my direct reports to communicate my expectations and work style and to learn their goals and work style.

❑   I have met with an HR manager at my company to get a clear
picture on the goals of the company and to establish a rapport
to get support on my goals for my tenure at the company. Or
as a business owner, have an updated business plan.

Your Going HARD baseline is the foundation to build on for your
professional success. It is essential you have a plan for your future and
are on the same page with anyone you are working with, whether aiming
for a promotion in two years or getting your apartment repaired.

As a Boss Bride, information is your friend. And when you lead with
your heart, you cannot lose.

Heart actions mean you are actively listening to what your heart desires on the regular. In 2009 my business cards for my job ran out and I
didn't ask for more. I had been a web editor for two and a half years grinding around the clock cranking out stories. I knew in my spirit change was
coming. Word of impending layoffs ran throughout the company and
was reported in *The New York Times*. One Monday the rumor hit that
layoffs were the next day. My team wondered if we would be affected.
That morning I got dressed in my favorite dress. In case I was getting
laid off, I wanted to look my best. I knew I was doing a good job but
head count is head count. Then the unexpected happened: most of my
team got the ax. As I was standing in the office of a coworker who had
just been cut, my phone rang. I ran over and it was my manager asking
me to his office. I grabbed my notebook and walked over with my head
high. I was told there was restructuring and my position had been eliminated. I didn't know what was coming next, but trusted good things were
on the way. I had friends call me like someone had died but I refused to
take the layoff as a setback. Less than a month after my last day I had
my second interview for a social media manager position in PR and was
offered the job. I was making more money and less stressed. I had time
to focus on the things I loved most and organized my own business.

Going HARD means defining each experience for yourself and being present in your life and choices. You always have a choice.

How many times have you been busy rushing through life and you forget your keys or wallet? By getting in control of your life instead of being overwhelmed, you are able to be effective. Going HARD means being intentional. I had to learn to stop being busy and get busy being efficient. It's what my business coach Jullien Gordon calls "slowing up"—slowing down to be more mindful and to get more accomplished through less effort.

Every decision we make impacts our destination, where we ultimately want to be. That's why it's so important that you are clear on your vision at all times, so you make choices that lead you to your desired destination.

Going to sleep with your makeup on. Skipping a workout. Taking your lunch to work. All the little decisions impact our futures. What you choose today impacts what's coming next.

And as a Boss Bride you will have more options than you realistically can commit to and will constantly need to flex your decision muscle and Go HARD with **H**eart **A**ctions and **R**esearched **D**ecisions.

Here are a few choices broken down to see how one decision can impact your destiny.

DECISION

You break a date in order to get a big work project done.

IMPACT

Since you are dating an understanding guy who knows workplace demands, he is disappointed but understands and doesn't try to make you feel bad or guilty.

DESTINATION

For your desire for a healthy relationship, it's important you communicate early and often when things change and manage your time effectively.

DECISION

You break another date that week at the last minute and then don't get in touch with him to re-schedule.

IMPACT

Now the man in your life wonders if his and your time together are a priority and questions if you are really interested. This relationship may be in jeopardy.

DESTINATION

You are disrespecting someone's time, something you wouldn't stand for if positions were reversed. You now have a habit of canceling on people, which can alienate the people you care about.

DECISION

Promotions are coming up soon. You make a deck with all of your accomplishments of the last year.

IMPACT

You still don't get promoted, but great slides.

DESTINATION

Still a win. It's important that you capture your impact and advocate for yourself as you plan your future moves.

DECISION

You see your manager's manager in the café and go over to strike up a conversation.

IMPACT

Your manager heard about this convo and asks what you talked about and why you didn't mention it.

DESTINATION

This is your career and it's important to cultivate relationships at every level. Chat away while also managing your relationship with your manager by keeping her or him in the loop.

DECISION

You find out you have to let someone go on your team. You deliver the news with care.

IMPACT

Your team is sad but supportive of the former team member, who is treated with dignity and respect.

DESTINATION

Integrity shows how we handle the things we don't want to handle. Karma is real. How you treat others generates how you are treated.

DECISION

A coworker steals credit for your idea in a meeting. You are shocked and don't say anything.

IMPACT

You feel hurt and minimize working with this sneaky colleague.

DESTINATION

You appreciate the lesson to own your ideas and take responsibility for how that person knew about your ideas before you shared in the first place.

DECISION

The new guy at work is cute and it's been a while since you've met an attractive guy. You ask him out to dinner to help him get acclimated. Two birds. One date.

IMPACT

You have officially offered your love life as water cooler conversation. Yes, your nosy coworkers are watching and gossiping.

DESTINATION

Whether he accepts or declines this can be used against you long after the dust of this love connection settles, impacting how you are viewed at the company.

Often we make decisions thinking of the short-term impact, and not always the lasting effect on our destination. Going HARD means thinking long term and from your heart. We spend the majority of our time working, yet aren't always being efficient with that time. Busy work that isn't connected to results, gossiping with coworkers, and saying yes to the wrong things can keep us late at work and not moving on our goals.

Your Smart Choice Cheat Sheet

If you are ever unsure if a decision is moving you toward your goals ask the following:

- Will this give me life?
- What is the impact in the short term?
- What is the impact in the long term?
- Who will be impacted by my choice?
- What does this choice cost me?
- When I close my eyes and let my spirit guide me, what is the right choice?

#BossBride Vow

- I will Go HARD with Heart Actions based on my goals for my future and Researched Decisions that propel me forward.

Often we make decisions without counting the cost. A smart choice moves you further toward your goal or helps you maintain your current position. What helps me not eat all the ice cream (sea salt, so tasty) and steer away from overbooking my schedule with fab events is I count the costs. I know my ultimate goals are to impact the world while enjoying what this planet has to offer in a healthy body.

And sometimes what's best for us may not be in the best interest of others. And that's okay.

As a Boss Bride you will often say no to things you like and people you like to say yes to something greater. Being willing to give up your good to create space for your great requires trust that better is always coming.

The Ring: RSVP No

Part of Going HARD is building your NO muscle so that you can show up more powerfully for things that are a priority. Knowing you, there is someone asking you to do something that isn't in alignment with your plans for the future. Tell them NO today.

Being a Boss Bride is going boldly toward joy and opportunity.

Exactly a week before this book was due to my editor, it was one of my favorite days of the year: Valentine's Day. And in true Boss Bride fashion, the biggest holiday of love was also a big day for my career.

I've always loved Valentine's Day, even on the many occasions I was not in a relationship. As a stationery lover (see our custom Boss Bride items at effiespaper.com), I loved giving out cards when I was growing up and continued that tradition when I started my career, giving cards out to coworkers and once hosting an epic Valentine's party at the office. Everybody wants to feel love. Galentine's is real and for almost a decade my girls and I have had a standing ladies-only V-Day event, our reminder that love is all around. This year was my first Valentine's Day with Sir Brooklyn. He surprised me by showing up at my place before I went to work and dropping off cupcakes, a teddy bear, and a card from the stationery gods at Papyrus. See why I keep him around?

Before heading to the office I went to a screening of *Girls Trip*. It's like *The Hangover* but this time it's four women rekindling their friendships at the Essence Festival in New Orleans, starring Queen Latifah and Jada Pinkett Smith. It is hilarious and if you watch closely you will see a brief appearance of little ol' me in the film interviewing Ne-Yo. As I was leaving the screening, I got an email from our editor-in-chief's assistant asking if I was coming in because our editor wanted to talk comps (read: compensation, as in somebody is about to get a raise). I told her I was on my way.

Once I got in and settled, I headed into my manager's office. She shared that I had been named senior editor.

I was grateful and excited! This is something I had dreamed about. I also have to add what I wasn't: surprised. My promotion was a culmination of Going **HARD**.

I had taken Heart Actions and leaned heavily on Researched Decisions. I had gathered information independently on salaries and promotions in my industry and at the company and leaned into my Love & Success Squad to make moves and develop a plan. I did the work and looked the part. I was unapologetic in celebrating my successes.

The coolest part was I had already been promoted—by me. The year before I stopped waiting on someone else to promote me. If my happiness was up to me and I desired a promotion, then I was enough to make it happen. After assessing my work and focusing on the core responsibilities of my position, I streamlined busy work that didn't lead to results. I was able to cut back my long hours to the hours I was actually getting paid to work. And I reinvested my personal time into myself. I was able to get an offer for this book, which means I promoted myself to author.

Two weeks before my promotion at work I was a contender for a cool position. It would be leading a team of eight to create sex and love content for a global audience of young women. After a headhunter reached out, I took the first interview and was excited for the possible new opportunity. As I moved to the second round of interviews, I thought it would be a good position and something I could even possibly leverage to get more money at my current gig if they counteroffered. And then I withdrew my name.

So why did I say "Thanks, but no thanks"? Well, although the site I would be working for was empowering for women, as I did my research on the position, I realized the parent company had practices that weren't in alignment with my personal values. I could not see myself working comfortably at the company. I didn't continue in the process to see if I would get the offer because I did not have time to waste on something I didn't ultimately want. And if I didn't really want the job it would be a gamble and game of chicken to go through the process to get an offer to hopefully tell my current employer I was leaving in hopes of them matching the salary. It's like an ultimatum in a relationship when you aren't really ready to walk away. It's manipulative and can leave you out in the cold. So I withdrew my name and protected my career karma. And I didn't need the offer to get a promotion as my other Heart Actions blossomed days later.

GOING HARD IN LOVE

As you transition into a serious relationship and married life, it's important that you continue to make Heart Actions and Researched Decisions in your career. The Working Wives share some of the new additions to their rules after "I do."

"I never do lunch dates with just myself and a male colleague. Perception is everything."

"As a married entrepreneur, I don't do night meetings at date-type places. For in-person meetings, I stick with daytime hours in places like coffee shops. I don't do this because my husband has a problem with it, but out of respect for him and the appearance of it."

"If you're going to take your spouse on a work trip, either bring someone else along like the kids or make sure he is self-sufficient."

To Go HARD effectively is to avoid going alone. One of the best places to Go HARD is your Love & Success Squad. These are people who move your life and career forward.

Owning you are the Boss of your life will also include managing others. I took a management course at my company Time Inc. and gained so much.

Through the course, I also became certified in behavioral interviewing. Hiring wrong in corporate is expensive. If you have a bad hire, it can take on average a year to replace them, after having the wrong person in place for three to nine months, then taking three months to hire someone new. Yes, a year without the right person on the job plus paying the wrong person and the time spent in hiring someone else is pretty expensive.

The trick to smart hiring, which can also apply to any relationship, including our partner, is to pay close attention. The biggest indicator of future performance: past performance.

As much as we hope people will change, unless they are truly committed to doing something different many of us are creatures of habit.

When interviewing people for your team, whether personal or professional, it's important to steer clear of what they would do and focus on what they have already done. That's the biggest sneak peek of what's to come.

Interview Cheat Sheet

- What have they already accomplished?
- How have they responded in the past to stressful experiences?
- Review examples of work
- Call references

One of the biggest breakthroughs I had in taking Heart Actions is realizing support is always around. The more you look to be supported, the more you are supported. I got a $5,000 raise without a single cent added to my check by taking better advantage of the benefits at my company. By slowing up I was able to expand my support in the company and learn about incredible opportunities and services (hello, onsite therapist, legal advice, and gym reimbursement). Going HARD includes maximizing every opportunity and service at your disposal. That also includes squeezing resources and insight out of the relationships surrounding you.

Ever been told you have lipstick on your teeth, something on your face, or toilet tissue on your shoe, only to realize more than three people saw you before this person and didn't say a word? Well, the person who shared the unpleasant news is a master of feedback and the others chose feeling comfortable over being of service.

Feedback Is Your Friend

Feedback is simply giving and receiving information on how people perceive one another.

According to our management course, effective feedback isn't general. It is:

- Specific
- Proactive
- Constructive

- Timely
- Relevant

Good feedback speaks to a specific incident and is information the recipient can use.

Feedback has fueled my career, giving me invaluable insight on how I am viewed and blind spots I may not be aware of from people I respect. Seeing how other people see me has also been sobering and helped me work on being consistent in how I want people to experience me. I got a load of feedback recently after experiencing a 360-degree feedback assessment where my coworkers, peers, and managers rated me in about fifty questions. I was anonymously given the information. It may sound scary, but it was one of the best gifts I ever received—to know how others felt about me. You never want to be in the dark about how people feel about you.

I also had to rate myself in each category to see where others agreed and disagreed on how I viewed myself. I encourage you to get clear on how you view yourself and rank yourself with some of the questions from Pilat.

ASSESS YOUR WORK SELF

Put one of the following next to each statement in the table below:

X = I'm nailing this
O = This isn't my strength
U = I'm proficient and/or doesn't apply

Working in a Wider Context
_ Knows the right people
_ Makes things happen in the organization
_ Rational and reasonable

Leadership
_ Inspires others
_ Adapts leadership style

_ Creates a team spirit
_ Develops practical plans
_ Constructively addresses shortfalls

Problem-Solving & Decision-Making
_ Takes responsibility
_ Analytical
_ Explores options
_ Makes timely decisions

Self-Management & Personal Motivation
_ Displays personal integrity
_ Makes use of time
_ Open and receptive
_ Supports colleagues

Achieving Results
_ Manages resources
_ Addresses shortfalls
_ Runs effective meetings
_ Demonstrates high performance

Communication
_ Actively listens
_ Willingly shares information
_ Persuades and influences others
_ Reduces conflict

All done? First, congrats on slowing up to check in with how you experience yourself at work.

Now take note of where you put an X, O, and U.

For the Xs, these are most likely your strengths. Notice trends and see if these are connected to your core job responsibilities. Also ask yourself, who knows if this is where I shine? It's not good enough to be great at something if no one knows it.

For the Os, these are growth opportunities in your life and blind spots to keep an eye on. Think about who is naturally good at these qualities and what you can learn.

For the Us, these are areas that may only take a little more effort to get to an X. Explore what tweaks you could make in your routine to elevate this experience.

Last, think about what is most important to your manager and clients, and pay attention to how you rated yourself. If you have an O in a category that matters to your manager, it may be impacting your ability to move up in the company, no matter how great your work is.

Because I had worked on being self-aware before my 360 assessment, there weren't many surprises in my results. My assessment also included written comments from my colleagues on what they perceived as my strengths and weaknesses.

One comment struck me the most:

"I haven't experienced this myself, but it's been said that Charreah can be someone that puts herself first, and if there's not something in it for her, she may not be as interested."

I could only smile after reading this because it had plenty of truth in it.

I had worked hard to get to a place where I was the number-one priority in my life. It made me a better employee, friend, and contributor to society to love me first, and then pour from my overflow.

The comment was a reminder that women are still conditioned to not put ourselves first and to put others before us, which can leave us vulnerable and depleted. I fly often and hear to put our own masks on first in case of emergency. And that can make people uncomfortable if we fall in love with ourselves and show up powerfully. I'm a living example that people will adjust.

Part of being the love of our lives and taking our place as CEO of our career makes it easier to hear what other people feel about you and it not have to be your truth.

Feedback is your friend. Seek it constantly. And commit to give feedback freely.

Save the Date: Feast on Feedback

Send an email to six to ten coworkers asking them to provide you with feedback to continue to grow. Copy text from the playbook available at www.bossbride.com/playbook.

Going HARD Gets You Home

The more you Go HARD the more you can go home. Many successful women have figured out that if you're the boss, you can set your own rules. At Arianna Huffington's Third Metric Conference a few years back, then *Cosmopolitan* editor-in-chief Joanna Coles broke down why you need to be the boss: "The higher you go in a corporation the easier it is. It's counterintuitive. You think you'll have more to do and it will be harder. The truth is you get more control."

United States Senator Kirsten Gillibrand cosigns. "People say, 'oh my goodness how can you be in politics with young children,'" she shared at a Women X Power event powered by *Time* and *Real Simple*. "The answer is because I make my own schedule. I remember having a family conflict where my sister was having a christening for her son in London and I had used up all of my vacation. I was very frustrated in a middle management job, with two weeks vacation. I borrowed vacation against the following year. I told the boss, I have to do this. She was a woman and said 'just know this pisses me off.' In that moment she lost all my loyalty and any effort I had to stay late. I knew in that moment I had to be the boss so I never had to ask someone for something that is actually reasonable. The more senior you get, the more money, support and control you get. That's what makes any of this notion of control or balance possible."

Going for your dreams and the biggest job can lead to more flexibility in your personal life. It's what Sheryl Sandberg lays out in her book *Lean In*. Commit to discover your double win.

I need you to do something important: take a deep breath in. And let it out. One more deep breath in. Now exhale.

Welcome home.

You've cracked how savvy women Go HARD. Now it's time you take full advantage of going home.

By putting work in its proper place you have time and energy to fuel your personal life the way it deserves.

Going home doesn't mean getting in your house exhausted from being overworked. It means tending to your personal passions, your body, your household, and your community. A part of Going HARD is to put as much energy and care into our personal lives as we do into our professional success.

Going Home Baseline Checklist

❑ I have a system or routine for tending to my household. That includes paying bills on time, cleaning, and purchasing items and groceries.

❑ I have a morning and evening routine of how I start and end my day for optimal energy and peace.

❑ I regularly spend time with the people I love most.

❑ I am friends with at least two people in my neighborhood or building to call on in case of emergency. (Yes, that means I have their number.)

❑ I eat meals regularly and cook for myself.

❑ I sleep at least seven hours most nights.

❑ I routinely see my doctors and dentist for preventive care and know what's going on with my body.

❑ I have a space in my home that gives me joy and has me excited to come home.

❑ I do an activity that brings me joy every month.

❑ I have a self-care routine where I regularly pamper my body.

❑ I have taken a real vacation in the last six months.

❑ I am on time for appointments.

Your baseline is a snapshot of what's working and the areas in your life that need more TLC. Anything you aren't rocking is priority number one in creating a life you love.

It's also important you define your SOSelfcare. These are signs that you aren't going home and caring for yourself enough.

My SOSelfcare sign is my nails. If my nails are looking rough it's usually a sign I have been on the go and run-down. And if my nails are rough, there's a chance a bill needs to be tended to and there's a follow-up exam with my doctor I have delayed.

Common SOSelfcare Signs

- Piled-up mail
- Skipped meals
- No time for working out
- Undone household chores

- Not sleeping
- Delayed personal grooming
- Eating junk food
- Paying bills late
- Missed appointments
- Often late
- Messy workplace or home

If any of these signs rings true, your life is not completely centered and your self-care is suffering. Self-care is not an act of pampering, but an act of survival, as Audre Lorde poignantly noted.

Save the Date: Self-Service

Commit to three things you can do immediately to up your satisfaction at home and love your space and your body. We do not have wealth without health.

Taking care of our home and body impacts our stress and physical health. As a cancer survivor, I am regularly reminded of how much of a gift it is to be alive and the importance of being proactive with our health and home life.

#BossBride Vow

- I vow to treat my body like a temple and to create a home that is calming and feeds my spirit. I will be proactive in scheduling time to renew and care for my body and spirit.

We can't Go HARD fully if we aren't going home. Not feeling our best means we aren't able to give our best. It also means we won't attract the best to us from partners and opportunities. I talked about that scene in *Girls Trip* where I'm featured. Well, so is my red bra strap. I was fresh out of a breakup at the time and did a last-minute job of packing, which meant some of my favorite undergarments didn't make it. There on the big screen was me and my red bra strap, which wasn't ideal for the dress.

Self-care is prioritizing your needs and giving yourself the time and attention you deserve. Going home for me is having time to tend to my personal chores and to go out with friends and do things that make me smile. It was a random Monday night when I met Sir Brooklyn. In my years of being a workaholic, I would never have met him because I would not have left work on time to have a fun and casual dinner. He can know me and love on me because I know me and loved on me by Going HARD *and* going home.

If you have been all in for your career, it may be difficult to automatically shift to going home. It may take adjusting as you start dating and building a relationship. As a Career Queen, I had to be conscious of carving time for my relationships.

Career Queens to Working Wives

A few Career Queens share how they adjusted to married life.

"I married later at age forty-three. During the first year of marriage I was on the road a lot, which made us miss each other and made me really guilty. I realized I had to shift my priorities to have more time for my marriage."

"Before marriage my career was my priority, but now my family is my priority. I work and I do my job well while at work. I do not take work home anymore. When I am home, my family gets my full attention."

"I had to learn to balance my ambition because it was negatively impacting my relationship and I was not giving him enough attention. I let my first business go because I spread myself too thin and he basically said it would eventually run him away."

The most satisfied Working Wives I interviewed treated their relationships like a business. They planned for the success of their union. They put in effort and created infrastructure in their home and relationships. They selected the best partner for their lives and business and built a system that worked. **The top tip from the Working Wives is to put all personal and professional obligations on the calendar and sync with your partner.** Here are their tried strategies for managing your relationship and career.

Plan Your Love

"I wake up every morning and make a commitment to my marriage. I don't take that for granted."

"Always involve your partner in your career plans because they are more affected by it than you may realize. Make time to ensure your partner is still an important priority."

"Set office hours. There has to be a time you are 'at work' and a time when you are 'at home.' Because I tend to work on the weekends, my clients think they are free to contact me at all times. I had to establish office hours so that I could dedicate time to my husband."

"Take at least fifteen minutes each day for yourself. Take time to love yourself; do something that brings joy to your heart. We are always pouring out to others and making sure everyone is okay and sometimes we are on the edge of falling apart. And because we know how to keep things together no one knows the war brewing inside. When we take time for ourselves, that's when you can give love, joy, care and concern out of what you have been filled with. You can't give what you don't have."

"Add date night to the calendar. Don't let your relationship get lost in the chaos of life. You must water your relationship for it to grow."

"We're slightly type A so we put everything on our calendar. We also use Asana [project-planning software] to manage major projects like our move from Houston to Oakland. We set annual goals for our finances and meet monthly to review our budget to ensure we're on target. Mint.com helps a lot with this."

"Call each night to say good night if you are out of town. When you focus on making your spouse feel the same way you want your customers to feel, your marriage wins."

"We send each other calendar invites for personal appointments like doctors' visits and car maintenance."

"I make sure I unplug from work between eight to ten every night to spend time with my love. We also plan weekend trips every other month with no work allowed."

"I have dinner every evening on my calendar with my hubby, and girls night out too. I also have my out-of-town trips on our fridge so my hubby knows when I am in and out of town."

"We don't bring work issues to our home unless it is something of major importance."

"No laptops in the bedroom. If I have to work at night, I take a break when he gets home to hear about his day and spend time before getting back to my workflow. I cook a couple times a week."

"If family is first, don't forget. Live by it because the job will gladly take your time, energy and sacrifice, then you go home tired, mad and beat down. That's when your relationship and love life break, which can easily lead to infidelity. You can climb the ladder without killing your home life."

Going Home Helped My Career

"The most important career decision you'll make is who you choose to marry."
　　　　　　　　　　　　　　　　　　　—Sheryl Sandberg

As the COO of Facebook, Sheryl Sandberg is the global messenger on the importance of women going full out in their careers with her book *Lean In* and movement of the same name. And she was vocal about the impact our personal lives have on our careers, reminding women that whom we love is a driving decision in success. And when you are strategic, your business and relationships can boost one another.

A study by Avon of thirty thousand women in thirty-three countries found that a supportive spouse or partner was the most important criterion for success in starting a business. As a Boss Bride, your relationship can be fuel for your career.

The Working Wives share how their partners positively impacted them professionally.

"With the support of someone that also believes in my future I have been able to live my personal and professional dreams."

"His willingness to support me when I started my company is part of what helped take our relationship to the next level. Our relationship has definitely forced me to try to find some stability in my professional life, especially as we look to having a family one day."

"We have worked together to help one another reach the next steps in our careers."

"We influenced one another to quit our careers and start our own businesses after being married for about two years and not being financially stable. We got married at a young age and started our family so it was important to us that we became financially stable by thirty. Now, we have several thriving businesses among the two of us and we're not even thirty yet."

"We share resources and contacts with one another and strategically plan attendance at networking events for optimal usage of time."

"I was more confident stepping out as an entrepreneur because my husband has a full-time job with benefits."

"Having the support of someone who really wants you to succeed is invaluable."

"We're best friends and both extremely driven so we feed off of each other. He's been an entrepreneur for over fifteen years and has pushed me to chase excellence in everything I do since starting my business."

"I started my doctorate the year we got married. We had no idea how much that would define our lives, financially and emotionally. Not long after graduating, I quit my full-time job for entrepreneurship. Being married gave me the consistent emotional support and financial safety net I needed to get started. A lot of our life together has been taken up by my big pursuits. We make planned time to be with each other without work being at the center."

"My career would not be the same without my husband's support, so making sure to acknowledge how important and critical he is to my success goes a long way. Since starting a business my husband has seen me do things he could not believe. He said watching me make my dreams come true made him fall more in love. I didn't realize how determined I was and he didn't either but seeing it gave him a new respect for me. That was something we never saw coming but a sweet reward."

"My professional pursuits and love life go hand in hand. I go after bigger goals now that I am in a loving relationship. I don't give up so easily now that I am in a loving relationship and I also feel supported which helped me to ask for help and even build a team. Before my marriage, I was a one-woman team that was stressed and burned out. Now I feel forced to take breaks, organize my days and nights better and take time for pleasure."

"My professional pursuits have caused my husband to see my value as a partner, not just as a typical wife. He values my opinion due to him seeing me as a success professionally. Having his support has allowed me to take more risk professionally. Both areas of my life have been positively impacted."

As you continue to unleash love in every area of your life, commit to Go HARD with smart Heart Actions, Researched Decisions, and go home.

Whispers of a Woman

WHAT EACH WORKING WIFE WOULD SAY TO HERSELF AS SHE WALKED DOWN THE AISLE

Remember that marriage is work, there will be sacrifices and compromises that you will need to make in order to maintain a long-term relationship. **You can do this!** Balance, let my spouse and children know that they are my priority.

Remember why you go so hard, remember what's most important. Marriage first, career second. **Love and support your husband, but don't lose yourself and aspirations in doing so. I can exist in this relationship and in my personal life.** I want this marriage for life. I only plan to work until fifty-five. **Always put God first.** It's important to remember we both want the same things no matter how we grow. **Your partner knows he's the heart of your life!** Build each other in being confident and pray for each other. **Don't sacrifice your friendships (both male and female) for marriage.** Make sure your partner knows they are a top priority—even over the pursuit of your career.

5

MIND YOUR BUSINESS

Trust your husband. Adore your husband. And get as much as you can in your own name.
—JOAN RIVERS

Love doesn't cost a thing. But to sustain your life and a happy relationship often takes cold hard cash and financial compatibility. As women, we have to manage our money and think for our futures. We are living longer and more likely to be financially responsible for children and/or aging parents.

In the book *Secrets of Six-Figure Women,* 85 percent of the women making six figures were married and credited their partners for a direct impact on their financial success.

Before we can talk about how money impacts your relationship, we first have to get clear on your own relationship with money. The better you are with money, the more you are prepared for the life you deserve and the less likely you will tolerate someone who is not good with money.

Meet Your Man, Money

Pop quiz: If your money were your man, how would your relationship be? Would you be happily married or sleeping in separate bedrooms? Would you know everything about him or be acquaintances that spent as little time together as possible?

When my friend Tonya Rapley of My Fab Finance asked about my relationship with money a few years ago, it was the first time I realized I had a relationship with money. We were at a New Year's event hosted by our business coach Jullien Gordon and I didn't like the answers that came to my mind. I tolerated money as a necessity but was distant. Money was like a step-uncle who married my favorite aunt and I was still figuring out if I liked him. At my worst, I was money's side chick. I took the bare minimum and asked few questions, while someone else got the perks of my hard work. I figured money would show up when I needed it but didn't have clear boundaries or expectations.

That distance and those decisions were expensive. I had enough to get by and make do but I didn't have a real plan for a financial future to build wealth and hadn't done everything I could do to understand my financial business and to maximize my money.

To chill the cold shoulder I had with my money I first had to acknowledge what got us there in the first place. Growing up in the church in the South as a woman, I had been conditioned to think that being motivated by money was greedy and that the love of money was the root of evil with scripture from the Bible like "It is easier for a camel to pass through the eye of a needle than for a rich man to enter the kingdom of God."

Once I looked in my past, it wasn't a surprise I kept money at an arm's distance. When I realized it was a form of love for myself and those I love to be connected to and responsible for my money, I could transform my relationship. I could value money for the resource it was without it running my life or being my source, just a powerful resource.

And even if you have been committed to making a lot of money and have amassed wealth (Get it!), you want to ensure your wealth is from a place of abundance, and not in reaction to what you didn't have as a child.

Now it's your turn to get clear on how you feel about money. Complete the "Dear Money" letter in your playbook and write down the current status of your relationship.

Include answers to the following:

- The first thing that comes to mind when I hear the word money is . . .
- My first memory of money is . . .
- Rich people are . . .
- The first time money let me down was . . .
- My relationship with money has evolved to . . .
- My commitment to this relationship moving forward is . . .

Sign and date your letter and make a note to have a money relationship check-in at least every six months.

#BossBride Vow

- I will respect money as a resource. I will stay in the driver's seat of my finances. I will embrace my birthright of abundance, including my finances.

Fall in Like with Money

"Money hangs with people who respect it." I clapped and tweeted when my mentor and friend Sylvia High said this at her I Am Woman conference in Atlanta. Many of us have been conditioned that talking about money and chasing dollars is greedy and evil, which is a lie. Seeking prosperity so you can be of the greatest service to the planet is responsible. Honoring money as a resource helps you unlock abundance.

You are worthy of everything you desire and the world needs more Boss Brides with wealth. Having financial abundance gives you access to options you may not otherwise have. You can pay for a second medical opinion, fly to a friend who has lost a loved one, and leave a bad relationship or job when you have managed your money right. Women are still making incredible gains in being empowered in their financial lives. It wasn't until 1974 that a woman could get a credit card without her husband's approval. You don't have to be in love with money to like and respect it. Here's how to be more empowered in your finances.

1. CALCULATE HOW MUCH IT COSTS TO BE YOU

When we end up with more month than money, we have not been honest about our costs and our cash. Determine how much money you spend on average and what you are spending it on. I have the Mint app on my phone, which helped me see where my money was going, set a realistic budget, and see the red flags in my spending. My big heart was paying for way too many mouths on my budget and those lunches and dinners add up quickly. I also realized after bills, savings, investments, rent, utilities, groceries, toiletries, phone, internet, and transportation, there was not as much money for good times as I imagined. Know your hard numbers of what you spend a month and how you spend it.

2. TALK MONEY

Because women are often conditioned to not chase money, we also aren't always as comfortable to talk money. That is an expensive mistake. I once found out someone doing a similar job to mine was making $20,000 more than I was. If I had done my part to talk money and gather information before accepting the role, I could have advocated for a salary closer to the company's rate before accepting. I eventually made up for the gap and have kept that lesson by often asking friends their salary and how much they charge for their services. People are way more willing to tell you or give you a range than you might think. And if they are not willing, that is totally fine. I challenge you to ask three friends their salary range. Talking money regularly builds your wealth muscle.

3. PAY YOURSELF

I have to tell you there is a feeling as good as that heart orgasm I told you about in Chapter 2: making your own money. It was thrilling and euphoric to see "direct deposit received" in my email after my first online course, Happily Ever Now. I had used my own talents to make my own money. And it was invigorating. Give yourself a goal of how much money you will make each quarter and wow yourself with the many ways you can get there.

4. GIFT YOURSELF GREAT CREDIT

Your future happiness and the house you take your babies home to is impacted by how you manage money and your credit score. We all are entitled to a free credit report annually from Equifax, Experian, and TransUnion. You can get one of the three reports quarterly to see your credit progress throughout the year. Creditkarma.com will share what is impacting your credit the most. You should not charge more than 30 percent of your credit line. Mint will also link your credit to your free account so you can see how your score changes. It felt amazing to be waiting on the train and get an email that my credit went up two points. #SmallWins count too!

5. AVOID IDENTITY THEFT

Having your identity stolen cannot only be a nightmare, but expensive. Update your passwords often and have unique words. As I was writing this book I used combinations with "Writedaily" and "finish strong" with numbers and punctuation to have passwords no one could guess and to give myself encouragement in finishing. Double win.

6. GET YOUR "GET MONEY" TEAM

Your Love & Success Squad needs people who help you build and manage wealth. Start with building a rapport with someone at your bank and researching a financial adviser to help you navigate.

BONUS: GIVE YOUR 10 PERCENT

Since the first chapter I've been saying abundance is your birthright. And part of tapping into my abundance happened when I started tithing: giving 10 percent of my income back to my church. The more I have given the more I have had to give. I have seen my relationship with money transform and my wealth grow by tapping into my higher power when it comes to every area of my life including my finances. Actively giving reminds us how much we already have and creates space for more.

Save the Date: A Date with Money

In the next week, sit down to review your current financial state, getting clear on income, debt, and expenses. Next commit to financial goals for the future and a strategy to get there. Check out the Mint app for a free and easy resource.

The Emotions in Our Money

Once you get an intimate relationship with money you are able to see and respect it as a resource for your life, and not something to chase, use as a crutch, or keep you down. Money has history in our lives.

High emotional intelligence—the ability to read the feelings of others—is tied to higher income.

And cleansing any past residue in our relationship with money sets us up for success and wealth, so we are not reacting to the past but building for our financial future.

Maximize Your Money

Once I got intimate with my money I realized it wasn't a Starbucks habit keeping me from wealth. It was the reality that I had fixed expenses living in expensive New York City and to start building wealth I needed to make more money.

As a Boss Bride, we have to maximize our earning potential and wealth. In Chapter 1 we talked about how we will have to stretch on our journey and leave our comfort zone. One of my stretches in spending was to get used to investing in myself and spending more for quality. Once I knew I was worthy of everything I desired, I spent a couple thousand dollars on training to be the best version of myself. And I've learned we can often afford what becomes important to us—and thinking wealthy creates wealth. With that came new relationships with people living the life I want to live and new opportunities. After pitching Bevy Smith to be on her Sirius Radio Show and telling her all my business the day before Valentine's Day, we took a cab ride together to Harlem, where we both live. She talked about being fresh from a trip to Los Angeles during awards season and how she budgeted to fly business class and stay in nice hotels for the caliber of people she meets. She had just booked Uzo Aduba for *Orange Is the New Black* after seeing her on a flight. That convo made me more intentional of accessing the power around me when I travel. I upgraded my travel credit card and now try to get to airports a little earlier to stop by the lounges and dress like the boss I am. On my flight back from South Africa I sat next to the country's chief statistician, who had handed President Nelson Mandela the first census report completed during his term. When we maximize our money we can spend it on incredible experiences and access.

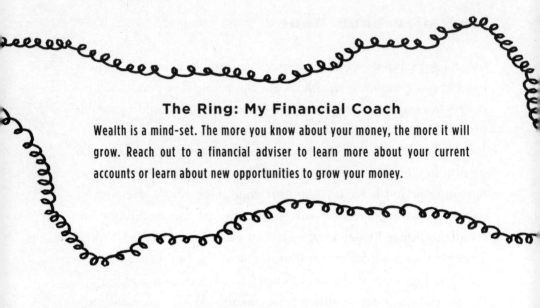

The Ring: My Financial Coach

Wealth is a mind-set. The more you know about your money, the more it will grow. Reach out to a financial adviser to learn more about your current accounts or learn about new opportunities to grow your money.

Wealth for Working Wives

The ladies share their best money secrets and lessons.

"I was encouraged to finish college before getting married and to know what direction I wanted to go as far as my career. I didn't know why it was important until years later in the marriage when we started having financial problems."

"We were counseled by a pastor before marriage to live off of one income and purchase a home on ONE income. We followed his advice and purchased a home off of my income only. Months after purchasing and before our wedding, my husband's position was terminated. Although he was given notice, this was devastating. Because we followed wise counsel, we were not in jeopardy financially. We made some shifts in our spending, but were never in jeopardy of losing our home. Live off one income!"

The women I interviewed had plenty to share on managing dollars with common sense.

BOSS BRIDE CONFESSIONS
MANAGE YOUR MONEY

One of my go-to Boss Brides for money matters is Lori Jones Gibbs. She's been married thirty-seven years and has more than thirty years working in financial services and it shows. At the Wealth Experience in Miami, she shared how she is leaving each of her four grandkids a trust fund of $100,000 they can spend toward college or a business. She is candid about the ways she and her husband have created wealth after growing up in public housing.

1. Stop trying to be like her. "Us Joneses have been faking it for years and you think we have it together. We don't. Don't live outside your means to be like people who don't have it either."

2. You need to have assets in your name. "I have a home and accounts in my name. If the gravy is not there from my husband, I still got the meat and the potatoes. If you manage your credit correctly it can turn into an asset."

3. You need an emergency fund. "You never know what's happening tomorrow. The higher your income, the longer it will take to find a comparable job. Go for twelve months of savings."

Be an Investor

One of the reasons the wealth of women remains lower than men is we are less likely to invest our money to grow it—and also less likely to be in a position to invest in the great businesses of other women. Grow your money by learning how to invest your hard-earned coins. Vanguard and Ellevest are two online sites you can invest with in minutes. I love Ellevest and joined because it's built for and by women, founded by Boss Bride and former Wall Street CEO Sallie Krawcheck.

Here are common wealth goals that Ellevest asks you to choose from to find your top financial priorities.

An emergency fund: Roofs leak. Birth control fails. Companies "rightsize." You'll sleep easier knowing you have a financial cushion to ease any bumps in the road.
Wealth check: More than 90 percent of professional women view building an emergency fund as important.

Yes, me!: "Yes, me!" is just what it sounds like—an investment in yourself. Building personal wealth is always a smart move, and it could give you more options in the future.
Wealth check: Nearly 70 percent of professional women have reinvented their career. And another 16 percent plan to do so.

Retirement on my terms: Your retirement should be the one you've always wanted, whether you head for warmer climates, around the world, a new career, or just your own front porch.
Wealth check: Just 1 percent of professional women plan to retire to a rocking chair on the porch.

A place to call home: Buying a home is perhaps the biggest purchase you'll ever make, and it all starts with the down payment.
Wealth check: Couples are still the majority of home buyers; number two is single females, at 18 percent.

Kids are awesome: They're also really expensive. Invest now so you can relax when it's time for preschool, summer camp, or even first homes and weddings.
Wealth check: The average cost of raising a child to age eighteen is approximately $245,340.

Start my own business: For some, there's nothing more rewarding than following your passion and launching your own business—make sure you're financially covered the whole way.
Wealth check: The number of women-owned businesses is growing at 1.5 times the national average.

A once-in-a-lifetime splurge: You've got your eye on something: a bucket-list vacation, a home renovation, a new addition to your art collection. Investing can put that within reach.
Wealth check: The number-one, dreamed-of splurge for professional women is travel, followed by a career break.

YES, you have enough money to start investing, even with pennies. Get in the habit now of learning and investing. Wonder how Lori is gifting her grandkids with $100,000 each? She became an avid and savvy investor.

Negotiate Like a Pro

Say it with me: Everything is negotiable.

In *Secrets of Six-Figure Women*, Victoria Collins shares how when she was a college professor in 1982, she learned that her male predecessor had been paid significantly more than she was getting. She asked the dean why and was told "Because a man has to support a family. And you're married." She shared, "I was totally satisfied with that answer. It made perfect sense. But eventually a little voice said there's something wrong." Equal work should receive equal pay. But we know that women still make only seventy-seven cents on every dollar a man makes for equal work, and that number is even lower for women of color. And as more women carry the financial weight of a family, it's even more important we get every dollar we are owed.

A Boss Bride is a negotiator—always advocating for herself and those around her. Most of the time we don't negotiate because of two reasons: we have not gathered enough information and we aren't clear on our worth.

One of the reasons the wage gap persists is too many women don't know they are being underpaid for the same work. The way we Go HARD in our careers includes Going HARD in negotiating. That's making Heart Actions, Researched Decisions.

Gather numbers to always know the industry and company salary ranges for positions. And have your three numbers ready in any negotiation: your ideal number, what you can live with, and the number you will walk away from. And whatever your ideal number, bump it up another 10 or 20 percent. Because the guy with a fraction of your experience is unafraid to ask for that number. It's much easier to negotiate up front than to take a position or deal and think you will catch up later. I have had to make up for the early years in my career when I didn't negotiate or even attempt to advocate for higher pay.

Negotiating isn't just about money but quality of life. There are Boss Brides who have negotiated for condensed workweeks, additional support, and sabbaticals. Always know your worth, establish value, and be willing to ask for what you want. And always go bigger than your first ask. If you aren't a little uncomfortable with what you are requesting, you aren't asking for enough.

Unconventional Coins

Whatever you love, someone is getting paid to do. After a decade of living in New York and working in media I've just about seen it all when it comes to careers. You can put professional in front of just about anything and someone is getting a check. Professional tea leaf reader. Professional chocolate taster. Professional hand model. Professional window dresser. Professional wine taster. Professional video gamer. Professional shopper. There are people who get paid to do any and everything.

Forget the old saying: Why pay for the cow when you can get the milk for free? Don't wait for a man to buy your cow or your milk. Buy your own cow—literally. My friend and graphic designer Clarissa Sparks of She Sparks Agency actually buys cows as an investment vehicle.

There are a million ways to make a dollar. Get creative in using all your skills and talents to make some cash.

Boss Lessons from Beyoncé

If ever you want additional inspiration in minding your business look no further than the reigning performer of our time, Beyoncé Knowles Carter. I experienced her sold-out Formation World Tour, which was also a master class in business.

#1 Leaders Leave Legacy

Though Beyoncé is the main event at her concert, she strategically shares her stage with other talented women. Screens project videos of some of the female performers she's signed to her Parkwood Entertainment label like fellow Texan Ingrid and Chloe & Halle. Montina Cooper of The Mamas, her backup singers, also has a new album called *Closer*. There were also solos throughout the show from dancers and her all-female band.

#2 Keep a Tight and Solid Team

The fact that I can say "I saw Julius" and many fans know who I am talking about tells us the levels of life Beyoncé is living. She keeps her team consistent, with many of her team members working with her for years. So I did see Julius, Bey's long-term bodyguard, carrying an empty garment bag as I was walking in the VIP entrance. And the reason I was walking in that entrance is because Beyoncé's publicist Yvette Noel-Schure is the ultimate Boss Bride, and has had Bey as a client for those 20 years. It's clear Mrs. Carter keeps a trusted circle around her.

#3 Diversify Your Revenue Streams

As we awaited Beyoncé's epic entrance with that hat to "Formation," videos ran of some of her businesses. There's Ivy Park, her fitness and athleisure apparel line, Chime for Change, the global campaign she co-founded to raise funds and awareness for girls and women, her company and record label Parkwood Entertainment, and Tidal, where she is an owner. Our icon is busy behind the stage and strategically aligns with causes and ventures that support her established brand, while not letting her central product—performing—suffer.

#4 Stay Grounded

"The most important relationship in life is the relationship you have with yourself. How you see yourself is how the world sees you," Beyoncé said before performing "Me, Myself and I." She has been open in the past about how she got pushback on her first solo album because none of the songs was thought to be a hit. It ended up being a banging success. She has continued to not let the opinions of others dictate her next move, both professionally and personally. Remembering why you got into business in the first place and trusting you are more than enough will keep any business strong when pushback comes.

Yes, You're Being Judged

Part of minding your business is to stay present to how you feel and aware of how others are interpreting you. Regardless of your relationship status, you will be judged by it at work and it can impact your finances.

In 2010 *ForbesWoman* collaborated with TheKnot.com and WeddingChannel.com to discover how getting married influenced women at work. The survey found that 29 percent of women replied an engagement ring would improve the woman's chances of being hired while 21 percent felt that it would be a negative influence on the interview's results; 50 percent of women answered an engagement ring wouldn't impact an interview.

One woman learned firsthand how an engagement ring can impact your career and shared her story with Levo League, a career advice site for women where I coach.

BOSS BRIDE CONFESSION: THE RING THAT ROCKED MY CAREER

"In 2008, I received a five-carat diamond engagement ring. It was the talk of the office! I mean, people stopped by to see it. I did not publicize it to my coworkers and simply wore it. I worked at a PR firm that fell on hard times. I was a top executive. Due to client departures, they made a round of layoffs and I was let go. My direct boss called me at home later that evening and told me I was not on the list initially, but the morning they made the layoffs, I was added to the list and was laid off. I do know the CFO had done a Google search on my fiancé. During the layoff, they told me it had nothing to do with my skills, and they knew out of all the employees, I'd be just fine and could survive it. I know it wasn't about work because I had just gotten a major client interviewed on the *Today* show! I also heard from numerous clients afterward that they heard I left to become a 'lady who lunches.' So, instead of telling people they laid me off, this PR firm instead told everyone I scored the husband jackpot and retired!"

It's incredibly unfair that her life circumstances were used against her. And she has every right to push back, especially if her former employer is misrepresenting her to clients. But it might be hard to prove wrongful termination. Most US companies have at-will employment policies, which means your position can be eliminated at any time, unless you have a contract or your termination was discriminatory or in retaliation.

Her story is our cautionary tale to stay abreast of the company culture and how we are perceived at work. Perception is still reality, so lead the discussion on what you want people to say about you. If you are concerned your relationship status is impacting how you are viewed, overcommunicate your commitment and illustrate your accomplishments. When your track record is stellar, other factors matter less.

Turns out, we also have to stay mindful of biases when interviewing or seeking new clients. Twenty-year human resources vet Kimberly Roden shared with Levo League what HR managers may be thinking when you come in to interview with a wedding ring. Here's what she shared on the site:

- Diamond engagement ring: "Will probably need time off for the wedding and honeymoon."

- Diamond ring with wedding band: "Wonder if there's a maternity leave in her future or little kids at home?"

- Gigantic diamond ring with wedding band: "Hubby must earn a good living so she doesn't need this job. Probably high maintenance and will whine or quit if she can't have her way."

Ouch. It's good to know what some hiring managers may think. It is also important to push back on making decisions for your personal joy based on the opinions of others. Wearing a ring and what style is between you and your spouse. Ideally hiring managers and job recruiters would focus on skill sets and not marital status. If it does come up or is an issue, that may be a sign this may not be the type of place you want to work for anyway.

While shopping for wedding dresses for my bestie and fellow lover of love, C. K. Alexander shared that she unapologetically took her engagement ring off while interviewing for jobs. "They are looking for someone to come in to work, not take a lot of time off to get married or have kids," she said. After getting hired and settling in to her graphic designer position, she wore her ring. "My manager noticed my ring and said, 'Oh, I didn't realize you were getting married.' I smiled and said, 'Yep.'"

One woman on the Boss Bride Advisory Council saw the judgment of becoming a fiancée firsthand: "When we first got engaged, several male mentors said, 'Congratulations! When's the wedding?' Then they'd ask, 'How many people are you going to have?' I'd say '150 to 180.' Their reply was 'Oh my gosh, that's huge!' and then not do business with me. They thought I was going to be planning the whole wedding by myself and it was going to distract me from my business completely. I worked right up until the wedding and the minute I got back from the honeymoon, and my husband and I planned the wedding together as partners. It was very frustrating to get pegged and lose business due to stereotypes that don't define me at all."

Not only are women sometimes judged because of their relationship status, sometimes they find themselves using a relationship as a defense after noticing the disparity between how single and married women are treated. As a journalist reporting on one of the biggest biotechnology industries, Claire Trageser, twenty-seven, found herself constantly hit on. She started wearing an engagement ring as a weapon in the workplace, and wrote about it in *Marie Claire*. Claire is far from the first woman to do so. She purchased the ring from Ms. Taken, a Seattle start-up that specializes in fake engagement rings, created by Katherine Lake and her husband. "We call it two carats of pure deception," Lake says. It's sad that patriarchy can be so strong that in order to fight off unwanted attention from men, women have to give the illusion of having a man. But as always, women are a step ahead, exploring solutions.

Married on the Job

After settling into marriage the judgment can continue. The Working Wives share how being married impacts them at work.

"I get asked about my ring a lot and if the price of it set us back."

"I appear more stable and accomplished compared to my peers. I have been given more responsibility and leadership opportunities."

"I have been hit on a lot by colleagues, even more now that I am married. Seems men feel safer knowing that you have as much at stake as they do."

"I moved to a less viable job market for my field to be with the love of my life."

"You can no longer have the 'work husband' or 'work wife.' That would be a recipe for allowing others into your marriage. It opens the door for what could be an appearance for infidelity."

"I got fired about four months before we got married. It put a strain on us to say the least. Before getting fired, my husband had already told me that I could pursue my business full-time. He has been a constant provider and has taught me how to have faith in him. He is committed to my success."

"I've had to compromise and haven't been able to move forward with possible promotions which would require relocation."

"I think long-term about what my family needs when reviewing new opportunities. It's not just about what I want, it's about what's best for us now and in the future."

"My husband has been my employee a few times on contract jobs."

As a Boss Bride who is passionate about your career, you will continue to Go HARD with Heart Actions and Researched Decisions as your responsibilities grow.

The profession and finances of you and your partner also impact the success of your relationship.

- Jobs with the lowest divorce rates are optometrists, members of the clergy, engineers, and podiatrists.
- Divorce rates are lower for those with higher-paying jobs than for lower-paying jobs.
- Law enforcement officers experience a high rate of divorce.

If you are in a high-stress work environment it's critical you stay focused on your objectives and communicate with your partner.

Water Your Love & Success Squad

Your relationships are especially important when it comes to minding your business. Commit to staying connected with the powerful people in your life so you can build equity for asks down the road. Send thank you and thinking of you notes. A little thoughtfulness can go a long way. And if you don't have five powerful people in your network, it's time to expand. Consider a professional women's group, an industry community, or counseling space. I joined The Wing in New York and have met some incredible women.

Men & Money

Barbara Stanny, the author of *Secrets of Six-Figure Women*, found herself sitting with a financial planner after her husband lost the inheritance left to her in bad investments. As you date to mate, you can use the Four Cs to assess your cash compatibility—and watch for signs of catastrophe.

The Four Cs for Financial Connection

1. **Circumstances:** What's his current salary and debt and what are yours?

2. **Characteristics:** What are your spending habits and approach to money?

3. **Compatibility:** How are you alike and different when it comes to spending and managing your finances? Are you both budgeters?

4. **Chemistry:** Is there a spark in how you spend together?

Just like in dating, the most crucial C is Characteristics. It's not how much we make but how we manage what we make that impacts financial health and our wealth. There are many people making six figures who barely have enough money for the month and those who make half of that who have a system in place to care for themselves and save for a rainy day (and rain is always on the horizon).

Get Intimate (Financially)

Financial intimacy minimizes the chances of financial infidelity. If you are serious enough to consider marriage, cohabitation, or having children, you are serious enough to know this person's salary, debt, and credit score. The opposite is financial infidelity, where couples hide their spending habits or financial status from their partner. Get in the habit up front of talking money. Many of the Working Wives have joint family accounts where they manage household expenses and separate accounts for personal items: a his, hers, and ours. There is no right or wrong formula but if you are comfortable enough to share your life and bed with someone, you should be comfortable enough to discuss finances openly.

As you work to upgrade your relationship with money, negotiate for yourself, and invest, your financial stock will definitely rise. And with that increases your chances of being a female breadwinner.

Female Breadwinners Survival Guide

Welcome to the modern world, where 40 percent of American households with children now have a woman bringing home the higher paycheck. In the past fifty years, the number of married moms earning more than their husbands has quadrupled, and the numbers continue to rise as women outnumber men in college and make gains at work. The growth of female breadwinners has outpaced our traditions and societal expectations. Making more doesn't have to wreak havoc on our relationships. It does mean you have to apply new rules to a new normal.

1. EMBRACE YOUR REALITY

One of the most important parts of being a female breadwinner is to honor your circumstances and plan accordingly. You do not have to hide or be ashamed of your role. Not all higher-earning ladies entered the relationship that way. "I see many couples where the man used to make more money and now they are adjusting to a new dynamic," says Atlanta relationship counselor Alduan Tartt, PhD. That was the case for Courtney, thirty-three, whose husband, Jared, a chef, lost his job when the restaurant where he worked closed months before they wed in 2010. "It was a tough transition for us, from him making more to me paying more of the bills," the Chicago makeup artist shares. "It also brought us closer. We had to talk more about our finances and future plans." As Jared started a dessert business, the couple got creative with their finances, mostly fueled by Courtney. One of their favorite memories is of a twelve-dollar date of putt-putt golf and Burger King's dollar menu.

2. RESIST OTHERS' OPINIONS

One of the biggest stresses for female breadwinners isn't the relationship, but what other people have to say. Step past what others may say and stay focused on your union. Times have changed and some people have the option to catch up or be left behind.

3. POOL YOUR RESOURCES

Psychologist Pamela considers her PhD and career success as belonging to both her and her husband since he worked various jobs, including one as a janitor, to support her when they wed and later while she was in school. "I am now the top earner in our relationship, and I wouldn't be here without his support," she says. "The money isn't mine or his, but ours. We pay the bills by working as a team." The couple who ate peanut butter sandwiches during their hardest times celebrated their twentieth anniversary in Rome last year with their daughter. "I can't put a value on my husband," Pamela says. Joining forces financially minimizes the focus on who makes what.

4. DISCUSS YOUR ROLES

"One of the biggest myths surrounding women who make more money is that we all want to wear the pants with our men," shared one breadwinner. "We are often leaders at work, but are also capable of following. We don't always want to be the head of the household." If you do want to take a break from leading when you get home, don't assume your man will know you left your manager role at work. Talk with your partner about the relationship responsibilities you each would like to handle. To assist your man in taking charge, let your feminine side show and ask his opinion on decisions. And to really push him to step up at the castle, let him know he's king. "When we hear 'king,' we'll do just about anything," Dr. Alduan Tartt says. "We need to hear that you trust us. Sometimes a woman has to overcommunicate to her man that even though she makes more money, she still needs him."

5. DISCOVER TRUE VALUE

We live in a materialistic society that can make it difficult to see the specialness of your relationship if it's not covered in bling. The most important items a partner can provide—affection, encouragement, laughter, loyalty—are not things that can be purchased. "My husband accepts me for who I am and would do anything for me," Ursuline says. "I can't put a price on our relationship." Instead of diamonds and dinners, many female top-earners are spoiled with support and a tidy home after a long day. Yes, there are men who pride themselves on how they support their wives.

6. PLAN AHEAD

Issues can arise in female breadwinner relationships when it's time to have some fun, especially travel. You may want a getaway and a Caribbean excursion is more of a stretch for your man than for you. Be willing to compromise on splurges that you both feel comfortable spending on.

Dating as a High Earner

If you are on the dating scene and curious if a new guy will be comfortable with you making more money, pay attention to how he talks about his job. "If work is how a man defines himself and what he talks the most about, he may not feel comfortable with a partner who has a more prominent position or makes more money," shares Farnoosh Torabi, female breadwinner and author of *When She Makes More: 10 Rules for Breadwinning Women*. "The couples that are most successful can transcend gender role expectations. When we were dating, my husband was up front that family was most important to him. He now equally splits caring for our newborn."

3 Habits to Avoid as a Female Breadwinner

1. Being your man's HR manager. You may see your mate's potential and have the contacts to help him. But remember: He is your man, not your mentee.

2. Weaponizing your money. In the middle of an argument, one breadwinner yelled at her husband, "My money is not yours!" She knew instantly she had crossed a line. "I now know that what comes into our home is for the both of us to help run our household. Just because I make more does not make me better or him less."

3. Hiding Your Success. Some high-earning women don't feel comfortable sharing they are shining at work when their partner isn't doing the same. But your good news may be the motivation your man needs.

BOSS BRIDE CONFESSIONS
CONFESSIONS OF A FAMOUS
FEMALE BREADWINNER

Jill Scott really is living her life like it's golden. In the midst of slaying stages around the country on tour with her fifth studio album *Woman*, she quietly wed her man Mike in 2016. At her sold-out show at the New Jersey Performing Arts Center in Newark she opened up on how her husband holds her down—starting with the clothes on her back. "Shout out to my man for ironing my clothes today. He's my partner and holds me down," Scott said with a grin.

Jill got real about the reality that almost half of American homes now have a female breadwinner. "Maybe the system is designed that women make more money than men these days," she shared. "There's balance in that. Maybe a man doesn't make a lot of money. Maybe he can iron a shirt. Maybe he can mow the lawn. Maybe he can get the kids up in the morning and make sure they have their homework together and you have a warm breakfast before work. Maybe when you get home you get broken off properly." And then she set the stage on fire singing.

Power of a Prenup

Whether you are the breadwinner or not, you should protect your bread with a prenuptial agreement to be clear on how money and assets will be handled if you split. At the Wealth Experience in Miami some of my favorite R&B singers talked about having to pay alimony after marrying for love to men who made less and were now having to hand over their hard-earned money. We saw the same thing with Mary J. Blige when she dealt with not only the end of her marriage, but having to fight to protect her fortune from her ex and former manager Kendu Isaacs.

An end to your marriage is sad enough without the stress of supporting an ex in the lifestyle you've introduced to him. Consider joining a growing number of women who get prenuptial agreements that state how assets will be divided if your relationship ends. Think of it like your car insurance policy: You pray you won't need it, but if the worst happens you will be glad you have it. On top of the devastation of a breakup, you don't want to have to part with your family's heirlooms, or be on the hook for someone else's student loans. You can also protect your current assets and future earnings with a prenup.

How Finances Can Ruin Your Romance

Experian, the global information services company and provider of credit reports, surveyed five hundred divorced men and women on how finances impacted their relationship. Those surveyed regretted not learning more about their future spouse's financial habits prior to walking down the aisle. Here are some of the stats I had to share:

- 59 percent of divorcees said that finances played a role in their divorces
- 71 percent of women and 60 percent of men said their former spouse's spending habits were different than what they anticipated before marriage
- 50 percent said their former spouse ran up credit card debt on joint accounts and 44 percent said their former spouse ruined their credit
- 54 percent said their former spouse spent too much money and that was the financial issue that played a role in their divorce
- 39 percent said the financial loss of a divorce had them not wanting to marry again
- Of those that are open to tying the knot again, 73 percent said good credit is an important quality for a potential spouse

Not only can finances rock the marriage, but the action of divorce can be its own financial burden. The average financial loss for ending a marriage is nearly $20,000 in cash and assets.

It's never too soon or too late to talk money with a partner or beau. I asked Sir Brooklyn in our third month of dating what his credit score was and how much debt he had. I also told him my numbers.

Update your playbook with your money goals and share with us at www.bossbridetribe.com.

Whispers of a Woman
WHAT EACH WORKING WIFE WOULD SAY TO HERSELF AS SHE WALKED DOWN THE AISLE

Don't do it yet, he doesn't have enough capital. Never borrow money. Save a lot, spend a little. **"Compromise" is not a dirty word.** You need to be loyal to your husband. You don't need to be loyal to your job. Because, unlike your husband, your job doesn't take a vow to be loyal to you. If you lose your job, your husband should be by your side. If you lose your husband, the only thing your job wants to know is how it will impact your work. **Keep your priorities straight.** Sex is important. **God, I commit us to you.** Put your relationship first, don't bring work stress home. **You got this.** Be always present in keeping your word. **Be kind. Even and especially when you are angry.** Knowing now what I wish I'd known then, I would have whispered, "Give me strength, and make me a better person through this experience." **Work together and say what you want.** Love is a choice. We have decided to love each other and make choices to support that. **You can always leave your job, but your husband is for life.** Stay true to what your heart says it needs.

6

MANAGE YOUR
MANY ROLES

How do we continue to be the wonderful loving spouses, the good mothers we want to be, on top of our game professionally and stay healthy and attractive? That's hard stuff to balance.
—MICHELLE OBAMA

One night while in office, President Barack Obama and First Lady Michelle decided to go for a casual dinner at a restaurant that wasn't too luxurious. When they were seated, the owner of the restaurant asked the president's Secret Service detail if he could speak to the First Lady in private. They obliged and Michelle had a conversation with the owner. Following this conversation Barack asked Michelle, "Why was he so interested in talking to you?" She mentioned that in her teenage years, they liked each other and briefly dated before she left for college. President Obama said, "So if you had married him, you would now be the owner of this lovely restaurant." Michelle responded, "No. If I had married him, he would now be the president."

Welp. Although this is an urban legend, it could easily be true, as President Obama often credits his wife for being the force that led him to the Oval Office. This story capturing the power of a woman's influence has been around for years. During President Bill Clinton's two terms the same story was used for Hillary.

And the tale stays around because there is much truth in the power the right partner has on your life and career.

You Are the Heartbeat of Your Home

Pop quiz: Move your head without using your neck.

That's right. Try to rotate or slightly alter your head without your neck. Perplexed? Still trying? You can stop now and admit that you can't. ☺

An African proverb says a man is the head of the family and the woman is the neck.

A smart woman is fine with her man being the head of the relationship, because she as the neck is guiding and shaping where things are going. She lets the head be the first line of defense protecting her while she drives to the destination.

I used to struggle with that whole head-of-house and submission conversation. I realized my discomfort was rooted in distrust. Once I learned to trust myself and my decisions, I found the freedom in following as I also lead with influence.

If you do your part to date like a pro, it's refreshing to let a powerful partner protect you while trusting your power to guide things.

Submission is not about giving power to a person but surrendering to your relationship and letting love lead you.

For a Boss Bride, allowing your man to be the head can be a breath of fresh air with everything you are up to. Women are also the heartbeat of the home, pulsing life through everything and everyone. As the woman of your house, you are a contagion and how you feel impacts everything else.

President Obama admits the impact of his First Lady. "Obviously I couldn't have done anything that I've done without Michelle," he shared during the final months of their eight-year term. "Not only has she been a great First Lady, she is just my rock. I count on her in so many ways every single day."

Barack and Michelle Obama. We've heard the story of the intern and supervisor becoming our president and First Lady. If you haven't already watched *Southside with You,* the film adaptation of their first date and Michelle stepping past the risks that come with dating someone junior on her team and finally giving Barry a chance, definitely watch it on Netflix. They are the epitome of a power couple but things weren't always smooth or easy. In the early 2000s they had a rough patch that could have derailed their relationship. It was shortly after their second daughter, Sasha, was born, and Michelle wasn't feeling how things were happening in the Obama household.

"My wife's anger toward me seemed barely contained. 'You only think about yourself,' she would tell me. 'I never thought I'd have to raise a family alone,'" Obama shared in his second book, *The Audacity of Hope.* Before national and international attention, the Obamas were building a life in Chicago, both with booming careers, and sometimes Michelle was the breadwinner.

"I went through [what] I see a lot of my friends go through, is how, as women, do we do all this?" she shared to CBS. "How do we continue to be the wonderful loving spouses, the good mothers we want to be, on top of our game professionally and stay healthy and attractive? That's hard stuff to balance."

The couple were able to rebound from the stressful time to strengthen their bond.

So what worked?

"Michelle was trying to figure out, okay, if the kids get sick why is it that she's the one who has to take time off of her job to go pick them up from school, as opposed to me? What I tried to do was to learn to be thoughtful enough and introspective enough that I wasn't always having to be told that things were unfair," President Obama said. The couple realized they couldn't wing raising a family, and their four Ivy League degrees would not magically make their home a smoothly running ship. They both committed to change. Barack paid closer attention to the household workload and Michelle created a system and communicated to her husband clear expectations while also hiring additional help. She also pursued her options at the office and shifted how she worked to adjust to the growing demands of her family. Their lives have only gotten busier since then but their peace has remained.

Most working women who start a family have a war story of the moment they realized things were no longer business as usual. For leadership expert Tiffany Dufu it was her first day at work after having her son, which she details in her book *Drop the Ball*: "I was so consumed with getting up to speed and running from meeting to meeting that by the time I realized I'd forgotten to pump, my breasts were engorged. With each passing minute they became more swollen and painful. Milk started leaking through my blouse onto my suit jacket. To add insult, the 'private room' I negotiated turned out to be a bathroom stall. I tried to pump but the machine suction couldn't latch on to what now appeared to be two throbbing balls."

She'd returned to work excited to continue her career as the Boss Bride she had been: on top of things at work and cooking dinner most nights for her and her husband. She thought a baby would smoothly adjust to the routine, that is, until she found herself in between meetings in the bathroom crying with breast milk on her silk blouse. Her sadness went to anger later that night when she got home and realized things were business as usual for her husband but her life had completely changed. She details in *Drop the Ball* how she negotiated with herself and her husband to create equality at home. The most crucial step was getting clear on what was important to her and her family and prioritizing focusing her energy in those areas. In a long car ride Tiffany and her husband, Kojo, got clear on four questions they would both say yes to before making a decision.

1) Will this advance women and/or sub-Saharan Africa?

2) Is this true to the values our parents instilled in us?

3) Will this put us on a path to financial freedom?

4) Will our descendants be proud of us?

Getting on the same page with your partner on how you will run your house is critical, especially as a Boss Bride. Although much progress has been made, women still do the majority of housework, leading to increased chances of burnout as we also make headway in the workforce.

Kill the Fantasy

What had Tiffany crying in the bathroom, Michelle Obama side-eyeing Barack, and holds many women prisoner is the fantasy we are fed that we are magical superheroes here to make fresh birthday cakes for kids, rock our careers, and be sexpots for our partners all in a day's work. What the Working Wives taught me is freedom and happiness live inside being realistic with what matters and making our own versions of what success looks like. That requires taking control and committing to change what we can change. One of the biggest shifts for Working Wives is to activate their marriage as a business.

By dating like a pro, you find a partner that is supportive of your career and willing to be fully involved in the success of your unit. And as a couple you can run your household like a start-up with clear communication and roles. What dooms many relationships is unstated expectations, which can lead to resentment. Silicon Valley executives Sharon Meers and Joanna Strober wrote *Getting to 50/50: How Working Parents Can Have It All*, detailing that women making strides at work is dependent on men doing more at home. The first step is for women to encourage men to be partners at home and do things their way, instead of leaving it all to us. "Done" is the goal, even with baby girl's braid a little lopsided and the cupcakes are from the store and not homemade. Release judgment on what things should look like and stay focused on your goals.

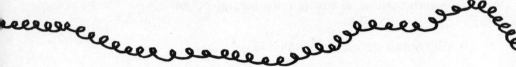

The Ring: Lean on Your Rabbit

Your Love & Success Squad includes your rabbit, someone who is five to ten steps ahead of you. Call your own Working Wife you admire to ask about her strategy for juggling a career and relationship. Some of her strategies may surprise you.

"There's no doubt that a lot of women identify with Michelle, because she's prototypical of women who came of age when they had career opportunities that didn't exist in the past, yet they continue to cherish and value their family lives," President Obama says of his Boss Bride Michelle.

First Lady Obama is clear on the many decisions women have to make impacting our destiny. "My generation of professional women are sort of waking up and realizing that we potentially may not be able to have it all—not at the same time," she said in an interview with *Essence*. "I know that I can't do it all. I cannot be involved in a presidential campaign, hold down a full-time senior-level position, get my kids to camp, and exercise and eat right. I know I can't do it all. So forgive me for being human, but I'm going to put it on the table. You've got to make trade-offs in life. I'm okay with that. I've come to realize I am sacrificing one set of things in my life for something else potentially really positive."

Sacrifice. The biggest testament of love is our willingness to give something up. When we are willing to sacrifice in pursuit of something greater, we are experiencing love at its purest form. Many Working Wives opened up on their strategic sacrifices in their career to discover love.

Love Wins

"When love knocked, I set aside professional endeavors and was able to resume them later in life. I have been able to balance knowing that family matters come first."

"My husband and I both met when we worked at competing stations in TV news. He was a reporter and I was a morning anchor. Five years later he's a flight attendant and I work two jobs. He could be anywhere from Ireland or Missouri, while I'm living the dream working in PR, at a church and my own internet ventures. It's work sometimes but we make it work. I make a point to prioritize time with him when he's home, even if it means cutting out other social opportunities."

"Early in the marriage I understood that time with my spouse is so important. I couldn't stay as late or run out at any time because the relationship deserved my attention and affection. So I always tried to respect my spouse's needs and desires."

"Dating great men was difficult due to my demanding former job. I tried Match.com and wound up meeting the best man of my lifetime. I left a six-figure job and successful career in music, so I could build a life with my husband and transition into entrepreneurship full-time."

"It was harder for me to get a job in San Francisco after graduate school in Chicago, so he promised we'd get engaged if I took my second or third job choice to move to where he was. He recognized the sacrifice I was making. We've been married three years."

Save the Date: Name Your Hats

Set a time to review your many responsibilities and roles. List all the people who depend on you for various roles and prioritize what is most important to you. As your load gets heavier, you will see what things you can release for a season.

Common Roles for a Boss Bride

- Family organizer
- Community and neighborhood leader
- Host of friends and family events
- Office supporter
- Wife
- Mother
- Work wife
- Trusted friend
- Sorority officer
- Adviser
- Organizer of social events
- Travel guide

As life happens your roles may change. Your career may explode as your romances fade and the reverse. It is important you consistently have open and honest conversations and make a plan together. One of the Working Wives shared how her career took off after she had been primarily available for her husband and kids. She had moved from a secretary to a leadership position that now included travel. Her husband was uneasy with the change at first. She started to invite him along on work trips so he could see her in action. Those "Take Your Husband to Work" days were pivotal for him to see how she had grown and the impact she was making at work. They made adjustments to their schedules and he became one of her career cheerleaders.

———

I went to Akron, Ohio, to see the christening of the latest Goodyear Blimp by local resident and Boss Bride Savannah James with her husband and sports legend, LeBron James, sitting front row. So often she had been a quiet force keeping their family unit strong. It was powerful to witness them tagging in as she took the stage and he sat in the crowd holding their young daughter with their two sons sitting close by. Later in our interview she opened up on their partnership. "I'm his support system with whatever he needs. The balance that I create in our house is for his success. How I support my husband is definitely how he supports me." Now that the family is back in their home state of Ohio, Savannah hosts a mentoring program to help teen girls.

Confessions of a Working Wife

One of my biggest Boss Bride inspirations and support to go full out for her career while taking care of her home is Mikki Taylor. The international style and beauty guru, *Essence* editor-at-large, and author includes First Lady Michelle Obama on a long list of legendary women she has styled and profiled. She is one of my rabbits—someone who shows me what my next season could be. At Restoration Weekend in the British Virgin Islands she shared relationship insights with us that I had to pass along.

1. Know Your Man
A lot of times we hallucinate about what's at home. I've been married thirty-four years and with this man forever. I know this man. I don't hallucinate about this man. I don't go watch a movie and say why don't you act like this. So much of life is programmed with perceived norms that it's very easy to lose your way about the gifts you have. We are human. Know who you married. If he's slow, he's been slow a long

time. Things aren't changing because you watched TV. The same man you married is the one that's at home. Don't get brand new.

2. Heal Your Hurt Places
If you had a limp, would you want to throw away that leg? No, you would do what you needed to for that leg if that was crutches or a boot. That leg is valuable to the whole of you. It's the same thing with your spouse. Work on areas of the relationship that are tender.

3. Don't Go to Bed Angry
The Bible says don't let the sun go down upon your wrath. When you lay down upset, here comes the enemy and then there are three people in the bed. Then you don't speak for days and you've got company. Talk to your partner and let go of any upset. Remember why you have been placed in each other's lives.

Don't Hallucinate About Who's at Home

That hit me in the gut. It is such an important reminder not to go looking for something or someone who is not there. Originally I had planned a section in this book called "Turn Your Clark Kent into Superman" on how women can bring out the best in the men in our lives. But the more I researched and lived I realized no matter how powerful we are as women, it's not our job to try to transform a man or anyone else. And the energy we would spend on trying, we should be spending on our own lives. What we can do is look to see if the best is already within the person we are with.

IS YOUR CLARK KENT A SUPERMAN?
In order for your Clark Kent to be a Superman, he'd have to already have the ability to fly. Here are signs your guy is a superhero.

He's a force of good: A Superman is powerful and honors his innate abilities to make the world and your world better. When he sees a problem, he doesn't wait for someone else to take charge; he does what he can to make things better.

He respects your hustle: Superman's first act of goodwill was saving Lois Lane, who was out doing her job as a news reporter. A Superman isn't threatened by a powerful woman and appreciates what she offers as she pursues her potential.

He acknowledges his kryptonite: Every superhero has a weakness, even Superman. If your Clark Kent is Superman he isn't ashamed of his shortcomings and acknowledges and manages his flaws.

He's adaptable: Life throws all of us curve balls. For a Superman that means always being ready for a change and facing life's challenges with strength.

You can inspire someone to cultivate and grow what they have, but you can't transform a man.

Listening to Your Partner

As women we often have girlfriends, mothers, sisters, hairdressers, and coworkers to listen as we lay down our burdens. Men don't often have as many confidants or spaces to share. We may have gotten ten compliments in a day from other women on how amazing we are and men often don't get the same. As the woman in your man's life, you are often a safe space. Here are a few questions to help you better understand the man in your life:

What's your dream?
We can get so caught up in the daily hustle, we forget to acknowledge the dreamer who lives in each of us. Hearing his goals out loud will give you a peek at the boy that once was and the man he hopes to be.

What are you afraid of?

Fear drives many decisions, especially for men, who feel pressure to live up to masculine ideals and our expectations. Connecting with his fears sheds light on his motivations.

What's your experience?

You can only see through your lens. Get his point of view on a topic or memory. While working to heal the dormant pain of my dad's absence during childhood last year, I was desperate to feel better and talked to my brother. While I was only a baby when our parents split, he could remember the day our dad moved out and what he was wearing. He also reminded me our journey made us who we are and I wouldn't be the person I am or have the life I have if anything were different. His perspective shifted mine instantly.

Why?

Whether why he feels a certain way or made a particular decision, get clarity on whatever you are unsure about, even if it's years later. My father moved to California when I was six. In my thirties, I asked him why. The answer didn't change that I missed him, but helped me understand him more and connect with his journey.

Silence and what's unsaid can be one of the loudest communicators. Starting conversations with our men strengthens our bonds.

Getting Out of Boss Mode

For many women, especially the Career Queens, we have been raised to Go HARD for our professional dreams but not groomed to be the heartbeat of our homes. On my flight to Amsterdam for the Europe Dating Awards and Conference I watched the Career Queen classic

The Devil Wears Prada. When I first watched this movie as an intern I paid attention to Andy Sachs, the young assistant getting her first break and dealing with a hellish boss. In my thirties I paid close attention to that boss, Miranda Priestly. Both ladies give the majority of their time and attention to their jobs. Andy's boyfriend tells her, "The person whose calls you always take, that's the relationship you are in," as she runs to fulfill an impossible task. It's her first job so we give her some slack, even if she is a stereotypically entitled millennial, and yes, I am a millennial. Miranda, on the other hand, is the editor-in-chief of the most influential fashion magazine in the world. And as powerful as she is in her career, her precision and attention to detail does not trickle into her love life. "I knew what everyone in that restaurant was thinking, 'There he is waiting on her again,'" her second husband says during an argument. It's only a matter of time before he asks to end the relationship during the busiest week of her year, Paris Fashion Week. Ouch. When people don't feel heard, they will let their actions speak up. "Another divorce splashed across Page Six," Miranda says. "Just imagine what they are going to write about me. The dragon lady. Career-obsessed snow queen drives away another Mr. Priestly." Miranda talked sweeter to colleagues than she did to her husband. Ask yourself: Who gets my sweetness?

As your relationship evolves, it's important to continue to prioritize love and not let those you love feel they are second string to your job. Your man should feel like the starting quarterback in your life.

As you take your place as the heart of your home, many women carve out what parts of their personality are prominent when they are at home and at work. The Working Wives shared how they shift between the two.

Work Me vs. Wife Me

"I let my hair down at home. I share emotions that I can trust him with. I feel freedom to be a dork."

"I grow professionally all the time. I improve my communication skills, time management and patience. In my relationship, I sometimes regress to old patterns that don't work as well and often have to remind myself to catch up to the new, more effective ways of relating."

"Very directive at work. Collaborate at home, where I am not the boss."

"I stand my ground for anything I truly believe in. In marriage, I believe that you must stand your ground firmly in the beginning to establish exactly who you are and what you expect from your mate. Don't be confrontational, but don't be a pushover. Your mate shouldn't have to guess where you stand on anything and they shouldn't find out where you stand just as you're headed out the door toward divorce."

"I try not to run the show so much when I am with my husband. I have to remember to make him feel like he is in charge. At the same time, I have to be true to myself and my personality. It's a balance."

"With us working together every day, when we are at work we are business partners and when we are at home we are husband and wife. However there may be times we sneak a kiss or two."

"I'm less of a hothead at work, but am equally passionate in both areas."

"When it comes to work I'm required to be on top of everything. When it comes to my partner it's kind of a 'fly by the night' sort of situation, which means anything goes to make sure he and I are happy, and I think this makes our relationship exciting."

"My husband allows me to be myself and also Gina, Marsha, and Nikita, those other sides of me that need to come out."

"I'm not as compromising when I'm in the workplace. When I make decisions I don't waiver. At home I'm quite the opposite."

"I tend to be more verbally combative with coworkers than with my partner."

"At work it's time for professionalism: I'm a boss and I have to handle my business. When I'm home my husband and I are partners in charge. We agree to share the responsibility of our family and home life."

"I swear more at work and not at home. I do use my calendar to keep work and marriage appointments. I'm very assertive in both environments."

"Everyone knows she comes first. She also met me at my own party and understood that my social life and my work life are almost the same."

"I keep the fire burning in the bedroom just as much as in the boardroom. As a public speaker I want him to see that same woman with her face beat, looking hot onstage, also at home while we are together. It is easy for that to fall to the wayside when you are so focused on your business and career."

"I am much less aggressive at home than I am at work. I'm more flexible at home and I try to really listen to my husband and respond accordingly. I used to jump down his neck at every turn, but life's short. I would rather enjoy his company and his comfort than to bicker over nonsense."

> **#BossBride Vow**
>
> - I vow to be intentional in how I show up at home with my partner and at work.
> - I vow to give the best of me to those I love most.

No matter how you choose to navigate your growing responsibilities remember you always have the ability to make choices on your own terms and you always have options. There is only one word mentioned twice on the cover of this book in all caps. Go look if you are inclined. That word is this: AND.

So often as women we are sold the lie of OR. You can be a career woman or a wife. Have money or a man. Be loving or successful. Do good in the world or be rich. The reality is AND is an option, even if it doesn't look how we expect it to.

Confessions of Couplepreneurs

One of my fave Boss Bride icons is Melissa McCarthy. She stole scenes and our hearts in *Bridesmaids* and has skyrocketed as one of Hollywood's brightest stars, nailing White House press secretary Sean "Spicey" Spicer on *Saturday Night Live* in 2017. And by her side has been her husband, Ben Falcone, who is her partner on and off set. "From the very first time we spoke, we were on the same page," Ben says of his wife in an interview with *People*. "We love each other, respect each other and try not to sweat the small stuff. And we really make each other laugh."

As fate would have it, the funny couple met in a Los Angeles comedy school in 1998 and married in 2005. They run their own production company and he directs many of her projects, often popping up for fun cameos and finagling a few onscreen kisses (he was the air marshal she bagged in *Bridesmaids*). It's a gamble to mix business and pleasure that has paid off big for the couple of more than a decade and parents of two daughters.

"Hollywood wants to make women so perfect," McCarthy said in her *Variety* cover story with her husband. "Perfect hair. Perfect job. Perfect manners. I know some of the most beautiful women, and they are so weird! That's what makes them funny and captivating."

There's magic in owning all of you. Working together also makes it much easier for them to raise their family. "I get scripts for stuff that she's not in," Falcone said in *Variety*. "We're here in Budapest. If it shoots in Austin or wherever, how am I going to see my kids? How do I leave my wife and kids for four months? It doesn't sound appealing."

The willingness to make rules, collaborate and tag out is essential for a couple with two careers. As your responsibilities expand, it's essential that you continue to plan for success. You cannot afford to waste time trying to figure things out when many women have already mastered managing a full load.

What's in a Name?

The Knot's annual gala is the wedding of the year, without an actual ceremony or couple. It's held at the New York Public Library (where Carrie Bradshaw almost got married) with never-ending champagne, a band, lavish dining stations, lush decor, and stunning floral arrangements floating in this historic building that holds first editions of classic books. For the 2016 gala it felt like being inside Wonderland if Alice were a couture-wearing Fifth Avenue fashion designer. There were men dressed for the gawds on stilts and a listening bar with headphones and caviar. For the special occasion I broke out one of my favorite accessories, a Kate Spade book-shaped clutch embossed with the play *Romeo and Juliet*.

Emblazoned on the back is a simple question from Shakespeare's play: *What's in a name?*

For a Boss Bride, that answer is: a lot. And as we go further in our careers and prepare for marriage later in life, we have to talk about the name change nongame. We are getting married later and achieving more professionally, making the notion of changing our name after "I do" have more impact. Women keeping their birth names surged in the 1970s with the women's rights movement and started to decline again in the eighties. In recent years the conversation and numbers have picked up again. According to Google data around 20 percent of women marrying keep their name after "I do" and another 10 percent hyphenate or keep their name professionally but may legally change it for their private lives.

As I started interviewing women for this book, I was blown away by the number of women who casually changed their names after marriage, many of them finding the solution to drop their middle name, make their last name their middle name, and take their husband's last name as their new last name.

Someone might get cut if you think I am about to give up my middle name, Katie. I was named for my great-grandmother Katie Williams O'Berry, an extraordinary woman who raised eight kids with her husband, was a straight shot with a rifle, and could grab a squirrel with her bare hands. I was fortunate to get to know her and she always had chocolate milk for her chocolate namesake. So when I hear people say, "I just dropped my middle name and I made my last name my middle name and took his last name," it doesn't seem like a quick fix at all and seems like more of an erasure. As we get married older, there can be a greater sense of pride in all we have achieved with our name.

In happy times with my former partner, we talked about married last names while walking to Sunday brunch on a fall day. I thought he didn't care since he previously expressed he wasn't that attached to his own last name. I was wrong. By the time I'd ordered shrimp and grits inside Chocolat in Harlem, he was laying out why the name mattered to a lot of men including him. "It's similar to how women see wedding and engagement rings," he said. "It's a sign to the world that we are united and committed to each other." I understood his point. I also believed that it was easy for men to be so clear on their stance because they weren't the ones automatically expected to change their identity and lose a part of themselves. Our patriarchal society had done us all in, and I told him just that. He made a valid argument on the simplicity of sharing a last name as a couple. I also let him know it was incredibly one-sided that the woman was often expected to give up her name. "I have worked very hard these last few years and my name means more to me now," I said.

I was also thinking about my aunt's Christmas card. The night before, while sitting in my leopard-print Snuggie, sipping ginger tea, and jamming to Christmas music, I had addressed my Christmas cards. I wrote out "Mrs." on my aunt's card and realized she wasn't a Mrs. anymore and had been divorced for more than twenty years. I then rewrote the card with a "Ms." For the first time it sunk in that it didn't matter what I put in front of her name on the card. She was still branded by her ex-husband with his last name. I understood why she and my mom kept their married names after divorce so that they would have the same last name as their children. I also realized how complicated the name game can be.

When I worked in PR, one of our execs went through a divorce. The emotional toll was grueling enough. And then she changed her email address back to her birth name and had to go through the process of letting people know about the new address and migrating emails, a daily reminder of where she was in life and the sacrifices she made for a marriage.

I was always unsure if I would want to change my name after marriage, only given pause as to the convenience of sharing a name with my kids one day. Inside there was no thought of what it could cost me—and no question that kids I would carry inside my own body would automatically not have my name.

One of the most fundamental rights we have as humans is to shape our identity and that starts with something simple: our names. Yet our society expects women to give up our birth names without a blink of an eye when we get married.

maiden

1. A girl or young woman, especially an unmarried one.
2. An over in which no runs are scored.

The truth is there is nothing "maiden" about my last name or yours. It is a name of people we share blood with. It is not unused and we are not little girls. I have used my name and have built a career on it, had sex with it, quit a job with it, fell in love with it, had heartache with it, seen the world with it, gossiped with it, been lied to with it, and lived my entire life up to now being a grown woman with this name.

I reached out to Cristina Lucia Stasia, PhD, Canadian feminist studies professor and former president of the Lucy Stone League. The women's rights organization was founded in 1921 and named in honor of the first woman in America to keep her name after marriage. Lucy Stone married in 1855. "My name is the symbol of my identity, which must not be lost," Stone said. Yes, it was a big deal and not always an option for women. For centuries women couldn't open a bank account or purchase a home without being married, and that included taking his name. When I reached out to Dr. Stasia, she was prepping for her five-year anniversary with her husband, whom she proposed to first. A few weeks later we talked and she blew my mind. In a nutshell: Put in SERIOUS thought before you automatically change your name when you marry.

BOSS BRIDE CHEAT SHEET: CONSIDER KEEPING YOUR NAME
Professor Cristina Lucia Stasia, PhD, schools us on the history of women changing our names after marriage and why you should put in thought before changing your identity.

The Backstory of "Mrs." and Name Changing
Women started taking men's names because they were their property. They were considered chattel. In the past men were called "master" before marriage, and they were called "mister" after marriage. Women were "miss" before marriage and "missus" after. We've dropped the "master" so men are all just "mister." But we still use "miss" and "missus" because we're so ob-

sessed with women's marital status. We still ultimately think that what de-fines a woman is marriage. We see that in pop culture. It's called her Big Day. When you call someone "missus," you're immediately showing their marital status.

Owning Our Names

It's ironic that couples will spend hours discussing wedding colors and whether to have a buffet or a seated dinner and a band or a DJ, but they don't have the most important discussion, which is about naming. Naming is who we are. There's power, culture, and history in names. When you want to go and look up your old high school friend, it's much more chal-lenging to do so if that friend is a woman because she may have taken her husband's name. She might even have taken her husband's name, gotten divorced, then changed it again to her second husband's name, so it be-comes complicated. That's really a reflection that we don't value the histo-ries of women, whereas with men, there's a nice, clear line that you can trace back. Men are defined by themselves, not by who they marry.

Unify Without Losing Yourself

We place too much value on having the same name as something that will unite us as a team. Names don't unite you as a team. Working to-gether, good communication, doing things together: That's what unites you as a team. If you're relying on names, it's a shallow Band-Aid for the real work that needs to go into a marriage to unite you. People always say that "We're a team" for changing names but let's think about teams. Teams unite without taking the last name of the captain. They're not known as the Gretzkys.

Fighting for Our Identity

Not all women have access to make name choice decisions. Even in the States and Canada, there are still barriers when women want to keep their own names. In many states, it's assumed the woman will take her husband's name. You'll get married and update that you are now mar-ried with your bank, lawyer, accountant, insurance, or other business accounts. You're not updating your name, because you're keeping it. In some states what happens is that they automatically update your name to your husband's name.

Pushing Back on Patriarchy

I still get mail addressed to Mrs. Michael Bowman. Every time I get a piece addressed as that, I just write "Return to Sender. No Mrs. Bowman here." It took my accountant five letters returned to him before he called me. He said, "I think we have the wrong address." He read it to me. I'm like, "That's right." He's like, "It keeps getting returned." I'm like, "Who did you address it to?" He's like, "Mrs. Michael Bowman." I'm like, "That person doesn't exist." It clicked for him in that moment.

Commit to the Conversation

Same-sex marriage has really shown straight people some other options, because if it's two women getting married or two men getting married, then they have to have an authentic, informed conversation about naming. They talk about things like, who identifies more with their family? What culture do we want our name to communicate and reflect on us? Where is our cultural investment? Whose name sounds better, even? Same-sex couples have those conversations. You can't default to who has the penis when you're deciding which name to take. There might be two penises. Peni? Whatever. If it's two men, you can't just default to the anatomy, but that's what we do in straight marriages. We're like, "Who has the penis? I'm taking his name." Anatomy should never be the basis of decision-making. Straight couples really need to have these conversations. My husband and I, we have different last names, but we are very strongly identified as a couple because we love each other and we hang out all the time. We don't need to have the same name to be identified as a united team.

Questions to consider before changing your name:

- Why did women start taking men's names?
- What's at stake if I take my husband's name?

- What attachment do I feel to my last name and what does my partner feel about his last name?
- What does changing my name mean for my culture, for my lineage, for the ability of people to contact me and look me up?
- In changing my name what am I telling my daughters and sons about a woman's value and who has the power in my relationship with my husband?

Your decision is personal, and should be a conscious choice. As women make more strides in our careers there will continue to be more at stake when changing our names as we earn more advanced degrees. Changing your name can also impact travel. When my cousin married in Italy a few years ago one of the guests almost missed the wedding because her passport had her birth name and her tickets were in her married name. She and her husband ended up missing the first two days of the trip in order for her to get paperwork to travel.

#BossBride Vow

- I vow to not succumb to society's expectation that I automatically change my name after marriage, but to think about what matters to me and have an informed conversation with my partner.

Society is evolving and there are men who are happy to have an equal. Dating as a feminist can be its own adventure as Dr. Stasia discovered:

When I was dating, I only wanted to date people who were progressive and men who thought that women were equal to them. From the get-go, I knew that my husband was a feminist. His favorite show is Buffy the Vampire Slayer. *We met online and my husband is also a doctor. He's an MD. I'm a PhD. It drives me crazy, because we'll go out. We'll be checking into a hotel, and they'll say, "Welcome, Dr. and Mrs. Bowman." Not only do they assume I have my husband's name, but my qualifications are now taken away and I'm just a wife. I'm "Mrs." I say that as a very proud wife, but that's certainly not my identity. He actually gets more frustrated than I do when I'm called Mrs., because we're still there as a culture. It's assumed that his partner has his last name. He intervenes in that all the time. I think that's important.*

When they were ready to get married, Dr. Stasia knew she wanted to pop the question.

I proposed to him. I think it's so ridiculous that we just assume that men will ask women to marry them and that men have to give up two months of their salary, or whatever the current going rate is. We didn't do the traditional thing. To buy the engagement ring and plan the proposal and then the woman wears the ring symbolizing again her relation to a man, while the man doesn't wear an engagement ring. And I think it's just really unequal, right? I found guys wanted to get married and I was focused on my PhD, my travels and pursuits. I was very happy. I was waiting for the guy who'd be patient enough to let me propose to him, to wait for me to be ready. I rented a room at the art gallery and I proposed to him there. Two weeks later he flew me to Paris to give me my ring. So we both have these moments where we both prepared something really special for each other and we both honored each other with the proposal. We both wore rings because I love him just as much as he loves me and we were so excited about being together. Men are jealous of him all the time. When they find out that I proposed to him, they ask to see his ring. It's really adorable, and then they say, "I wish someone would do that for me." We assume men don't want romance, care, attention or validation. But of course they do, they're people too, right?

I warned you Dr. Stasia is the truth. She is the ultimate Boss Bride, turning patriarchy on its head while preserving romance and the power of love.

Once you remove the blindfolds of the assumption that women will take their husbands' names after marriage, you see the ways it is sexist and shortchanges women.

We saw it with Secretary of State Hillary Rodham Clinton, who was Hillary Rodham when she married and when Bill Clinton was elected governor of Arkansas. It got a lot of attention. "It was a personal decision, a small gesture to acknowledge that while I was committed to our union, I was still me. I was also being practical. By the time we married, I was teaching, trying cases, publishing and speaking as Hillary Rodham," Hillary says in her memoir *Living History*. She later learned some people didn't like getting invitations from "Governor Bill Clinton and Hillary Rodham" and that the birth announcement for Chelsea Clinton got a lot of attention. "I decided it was more important for Bill to be governor again than for me to keep my maiden name," she states. "So when Bill announced his run for another term on Chelsea's second birthday, I began calling myself Hillary Rodham Clinton." And that's how she was introduced on the global stage as First Lady of the United States. By the time she was a senator, "HRC" went to "Hillary Clinton" and that's how she was listed as candidate for president of the United States. These were all her own conscious choices in a society that pushes women to conform at every level.

Chancellor of Germany Angela Merkel is undoubtedly one of the most powerful people in the world and possibly the most powerful woman, as the highest ranking female official impacting democracy, and was *Time*'s Person of the Year in 2015. She married her husband, Joachim Sauer, an accomplished quantum chemist, in 1981. They met while she was a research scientist and had recently completed a doctorate in physical chemistry.

So did Angela keep her name after marriage? Not exactly. Merkel is actually the last name of her first husband, Ulrich. She married at age twenty-three and divorced five years later. The most powerful woman in politics has the last name of a man she divorced more than thirty years ago.

She ascended to greatness and is the reason the name Merkel is known, yet it is not tied to the name of her family nor to her current partner. Owning our names is about us owning our power. You may impact the entire world and you want to do that with a name that means something to you.

This current movement for the advancement of women will also have to include reclaiming our names.

THE COST OF CHANGING YOUR NAME

Keeping your maiden name can also mean more money. A Dutch study found that women who retain their name after marriage are considered more career-minded and are likely to make more money. Tilburg University professors compared 2,400 women and found 75 percent changed their names, 7 percent hyphenated, and the remaining women kept their names. Those women on average worked more, had higher education levels, and higher salaries. The researchers also conducted studies to see how people judged a married couple when the wife shared a last name with her husband and when she did not. The exact same woman with a retained name was seen as more competent and intelligent. The study also found women who kept their name after marriage were often offered a higher paying job, which led to an additional $524,000 over a lifetime.

Since the nineties women changing their names after marriage has risen and steadily increased on Facebook for women in all age groups. Getting married is a beautiful thing, but does not signal an end to the woman you always were.

No matter what you decide, the decision of your name is all yours. As a Boss Bride, that means making a conscious choice.

BOSS BRIDE CONFESSIONS
GABRIELLE UNION ON MARRIED LIFE

Like many of us I have been crushing on Gabrielle Union since *Bring It On*. She is one of Hollywood's reigning Boss Brides. She has built a solid career and a marriage and family with NBA star Dwyane Wade, produces projects, and keeps our favorite stars as her real friends. I caught up with our girl Gabby a year after her wedding for Essence.com to discuss how she prepared for marriage, manages her family, and the importance of creating our own happiness. Here's snippets of what she shared.

PREPARING FOR MARRIAGE

"We asked a lot of questions and we keep happy married people around us. People are like, 'What's the secret?' I'm like, 'The secret is understanding there is no secret.' You just got to figure it out every day. We want to be around people who really truly love each other, that are highly functioning happy couples. We keep a lot of those in our circles."

SURVIVING YOUR RELATIONSHIP'S ROCKY SEASON

"My parents were divorced after thirty years of marriage. They never made it my problem. What they did was put us first. My mom just moved around the corner from my dad in Arizona so the grandkids wouldn't have to be separated during the summers or holidays. I'm sure that may be uncomfortable. All they did was provide a solution. I stay focused on what matters. Even with my ex-husband, we didn't have kids but I loved his family and he loved mine. If you make their peace of mind a priority, you don't need to air every piece of dirty laundry. It's nobody's business. You move on with respect.

Whispers of a Woman

WHAT EACH WORKING WIFE WOULD SAY TO HERSELF AS SHE WALKED DOWN THE AISLE

Your marriage and career both require support and attention at different times and involves another person when married. Give yourself space to tend to each, but don't stress if they're not each progressing at the same pace.

Keep God first and don't sacrifice my marriage for career. **Don't lose yourself, overcommunicate if necessary.** Remember to make sure he knows that he's more important than your job! **It's very challenging to manage it all, just remember to take time for yourself!** There's this idea that every woman should "lean in," but to each her own. People constantly asked me, "How do you do it all?" And the truth is, I don't. If I'm doing really well in one aspect of my life, chances are I'm dropping the ball in another. Don't get so swept up in your career, #SideHustle, and volunteering/mentoring that you neglect your marriage and take your husband for granted. **Ensure you're both on the same page concerning God and the roles others will have in your relationship and finances.**

7

TEND TO YOUR TICKING CLOCK—AND SEX DRIVE

On that independent shit, trade it all for a husband and some kids.
—KANYE WEST (PRE-KRAY)

No woman gets an orgasm from shining the kitchen floor.
—BETTY FRIEDAN

I have some news for you, which I will deliver Maury Povich style.

When it comes to you, fabulous Boss Bride, your real mother is kinda your grandmother.

That's right. While your mom was growing in her mom's belly, her little ovaries were growing with the egg that one day became you. And when you entered this world kicking and screaming—and within weeks of your first pair of earrings if your mother was like mine—your baby ovaries carried around two million eggs: all the eggs you will have for your lifetime. With all the science and new research surrounding women's fertility, it is important to know we are born with all the eggs we will ever have biologically.

By puberty, we have around three hundred thousand eggs and lose roughly one thousand of them each month going forward—until they are all gone. While we were getting ready for senior prom, skip days, and college essays, our fertility peaked around age eighteen. As I write to you in my thirties, it is sobering to realize my teenage sister has a higher chance of getting pregnant than I do. But all is not lost. We just have to be honest about our reality to have the lives we dream about.

Thirty-five is the average age a woman's egg health and fertility begin their steady decline, according to the National Institutes of Health. As a proud feminist, there is still no way around the fact that our beautiful and dynamic bodies have optimal and finite fertility. And the peak years to have babies are some of our best years to grow our careers.

Boss Bride, it's time to answer a question: Do you want to be a biological mother?

There is no wrong answer. But if you do want to be a biological mom the best thing you can do for yourself and your future children is to plan for it—even if their dad has not entered the picture yet. I've seen the angst of women approaching forty starting to wonder if their motherhood dreams will come true. I've also had the "don't be me" conversations with women in their forties who wish they had slowed down to make their motherhood desires a reality.

As TV show host, *InStyle* ambassador, and my mentor Tai Beauchamp celebrated turning thirty-five with a spa day in 2013, the American Society for Reproductive Medicine was lifting the "experimental" label from egg freezing. In the past, "oocytes," the medical term for a woman's eggs, had been much more difficult to freeze than sperm or embryos (eggs fertilized with sperm). Recent breakthroughs have vastly increased the success of preserving a woman's egg for future pregnancies. With egg age being a leading factor for woman's infertility, the ability to stop egg aging through freezing is a major breakthrough for women to extend their ability to conceive.

This is our fertility revolution, ladies. An option to hit the snooze button on our biological clocks and gain extra time to start a family, if we so choose.

At an Essence Festival dinner in 2013, Tai leaned over to tell me she was freezing her eggs. She was the first woman I knew personally who was doing it and I wanted to know all about it. I wrote about her experience for *Essence* in a piece titled "The Baby Rain Check" that was picked up by *Time* magazine and *Good Morning America*.

Tai had answered the question of if she wanted biological children with a resounding "YES." For her thirty-fifth birthday, she gave herself a special gift: She had ten of her own healthy eggs frozen to preserve her chance to start a family in the future. Tai's gynecologist first gave her the nudge to protect her fertility. "My doctor pointed out that I was at the age of egg maturation and doing well professionally," she remembers. "She asked why not go ahead and have kids now? My answer was because I didn't have a life partner."

Ever since Tai approached thirty, friends had advised her to consider freezing her eggs. "I have friends who got married later in life and have had their own personal struggles with getting pregnant," she shares. One of those friends that encouraged Tai to freeze her eggs was Elayne Fluker, creator of chicrebellion.tv and the *Support Is Sexy* podcast. Elayne had frozen her eggs right after her thirty-ninth birthday. "I'm very happy I did it," says Fluker, now forty-one. "Tai is a few years younger than me, so when I was going through the process I urged her to do it and do it now."

Tai's insurance covered her first consultation with Jamie L. Morris, MD, of Reproductive Medicine Associates of New Jersey. Each week Dr. Morris counsels women on every aspect of the process, including the center's 90 percent survival rate for eggs after they are frozen, as well as pregnancy rates for women who have used frozen eggs.

Tai paid $3,000 out of pocket for blood work to find out whether her eggs were healthy enough to move forward. Armed with a positive test result, she marked her calendar to complete egg retrieval, which can take up to three weeks.

Normally a woman's body releases one egg during each menstrual cycle. For "oocyte cryopreservation," the medical term for egg freezing, several eggs are required to increase the odds of successfully becoming pregnant later. Beauchamp injected herself with three hormone shots daily to stimulate her ovaries to release more eggs at a faster rate.

These daily injections, which are typically administered for eight to fifteen days, are not without side effects. "I felt like a basket case," Tai says. "I was irritated and bloated, I had a backache and my skin was so sensitive because my ovaries were inflated and full of eggs."

Tai discovered that the heavy dose of hormones also came at an emotional cost. As she rode the subway one day, she felt tears roll down her cheeks. "I put my sunglasses on, took my middle finger and dotted underneath my eyes so my concealer wouldn't run," she says. "It's easy to start feeling sorry for yourself in the moment, but I am so happy I did this."

After Tai endured twelve days of shots, her eggs were ready to be harvested. She was given general anesthesia, and during the outpatient procedure her eggs were retrieved vaginally. The surgery yielded twelve eggs and, after closer examination, the healthiest ten were selected for freezing. "Going into it I felt resolved; doing it I felt crazy; after it I felt even more empowered," she says.

"If my daughter gets to thirty-five and she has a desire to have a child and has not found Mr. Right, I would definitely recommend that she consider oocyte freezing," Morehouse School of Medicine President and Dean Valerie Montgomery Rice, MD, shared.

The Doctor Will See You Now

Tai's doctor also became my fertility doctor. At thirty-one it was time I checked in on my own ovaries and the health of my eggs. After speaking with my gynecologist she recommended I go to a fertility specialist and I remembered Dr. Morris. I took the train out to Morristown, New Jersey, feeling optimistic. I walked into Dr. Morris's office at RMANJ and sat across from her large mahogany brown desk. Pictures of her kids, born after thirty-eight, sat on her bookshelf and gave hope to me and the hundreds of women she had counseled over the years. In her office she detailed the process of egg freezing and IVF. Both processes start the same. You inject yourself with hormones to speed up your body's natural cycle of growing a few large eggs in each ovary each month. For both procedures, the eggs are removed. For egg freezing, your healthy eggs are frozen and kept ready for future use. For IVF, eggs are fertilized with sperm and implanted back into a woman for pregnancy, or frozen as embryos.

I first talked to Dr. Morris two summers before while writing about egg freezing and Tai's story. She was on vacation with her husband and kids. Even as a leading doctor in fertility helping women, she herself juggled her ambition and personal life dreams.

BOSS BRIDE CONFESSIONS
THE FERTILITY DOCTOR

RMANJ physician Jamie L. Morris, MD, is a leading fertility specialist and board member of the Society of Reproductive Endocrinologists and Infertility.

HER JOURNEY

"I have two kids, my daughter is five and my son almost eight, going on nineteen. What's really interesting is that fertility time is usually when most women are working on their career, no matter what career they have. The time frame where your best fertility is, that's usually your career-building time. I understand both sides, from being a doctor in this field but also being a woman who put her career first for a while, and a lot of these other things on the back burner. There are a lot of highly successful, highly ambitious women working extremely hard at their careers, but who also want to make sure that they are able to have all the other parts and pieces to their lives as well. I can certainly relate to that. I got married at thirty-seven and a half, and these technologies weren't available to me when I got married, which was ten years ago. I'm lucky that I was able to have my family."

YOUR OPTIONS

"Most patients are really coming in in their middle thirties. Some even in their early forties saying, 'Wow, I really want to have a child in the future. What are my options?' When you start to talk to these women you say, 'Your options are we could get you pregnant now with donor sperm, we could make embryos with donor sperm, or we could freeze your eggs.' The freezing of the eggs option is so great in that it allows future sperm. Honestly, we're not going to do a whole lot to change the biologic clock. Maybe twenty years from now we may have some gene that we'll be able to turn on and turn off so we can stop losing our eggs every month, but we don't have that now. It's either use it or preserve it now. The actual process takes about two weeks from the start of the in vitro cycle to the point of doing egg retrieval. It's amazing how empowered you can make women when you start to realize we do have options available."

HER MESSAGE TO BOSS BRIDES

"In a perfect world when every woman goes to their yearly gynecology visit they should be discussing their future fertility. If your doctor doesn't and you know you want to have kids, definitely bring it up. Know your body."

During my appointment with Dr. Morris we were nearing close friends when she suggested an ultrasound to check my ovaries. I was excited and thought it would be like on TV: she'd put jelly on my belly and slide a scanner across my stomach to see. Not so much. With no baby in my womb and my eggs being microscopic she took the southern route and stuck a phallic-like foreign object inside me to better see my reproductive organs. It was the most action my love below had seen in months following my breakup. "This is your uterus. Here's your right ovary," she said as I looked at a screen. "I can see about three eggs. Let's look for the other ovary. It looks like you have cysts. This could be your ovary or a fibroid. Has anyone told you that you have fibroids? Let's get an MRI to be sure." That optimism I walked in with? It slid to the floor. A few weeks later I headed to my MRI to see if I had cysts or fibroids surrounding my ovaries. Before I could lie down in a loud spaceship hub left behind from a stalled mission, a nurse pulled me to the side and handed me a tampon. These appointments are always poking. I survived and joined a majority of women diagnosed with fibroids.

On my follow-up appointment with Dr. Morris she told me my anti-Müllerian hormone (AMH) was on the lower side, which was an indicator of the health of my ovarian reserve. All those jokes about being an old soul had shown up in my ovaries, as my egg health had peaked. I could still have children, although I was advised to prioritize it and do it sooner than later or freeze my eggs.

This isn't what I wanted to share in a book, but I had to because I had never heard about AMH until I learned mine had peaked through a simple blood test. If having biological children is a goal, get to your gynecologist and ask for your anti-Müllerian hormone (AMH) as well as follicle-stimulating hormone (FSH) levels, which can be indicators of your fertility.

#BossBride Vow

- I vow to take responsibility for my fertility and to learn about my body and options if motherhood is what I desire.

The Costs

Of course, the financial obligation that comes with preserving your fertility can be a major roadblock. The total procedure for egg freezing can average between $7,000 and $20,000. Since the service is elective, most insurance companies cover only a small portion of the bill. I was open to pursuing egg freezing. During a call with the financial office for RMANJ I learned my insurance plan provided $20,000 toward infertility treatments, like IVF. Nice. But for an egg freezing procedure (to preserve my eggs without fertilizing them with sperm) my insurance, like many insurance plans, covered nothing. I had to be trying to have a baby to get financial support instead of being proactive to preserve my fertility by saving my best eggs for when I was ready to have a baby. And if I froze my eggs on my own and later wanted to use them for IVF that $20,000 of insurance dollars could not be used for those eggs. It sucks that more major insurance plans don't cover egg freezing but more companies, especially in the tech space, are offering coverage for egg freezing, including Spotify, Amazon, JP Morgan Chase, Google, Microsoft, Wayfair, and Citigroup.

In total, Tai estimates she spent $15,000 for medical visits, prescriptions, and the procedures. She also pays $1,200 each year to maintain her frozen eggs. "I'm already paying rent for my children," she shares with a laugh.

Elayne Fluker used the flexible spending account option in her company's health insurance plan to pay $5,000 of her bill with money taken out of her salary pretax. "You have to look at what your options are and be savvy just like with everything else," the entrepreneur says. "There are often legal creative ways to figure out how to pay for what you need."

There is even a layaway-style service for your eggs. Using Fertility Authority (www.fertilityauthority.com), women can put down a deposit and pay around $250 a month for two years for the service. The organization also negotiates with clinics for the best rates.

Once a single woman hits her thirties and hopes to have children, the dating scene can begin to feel like a stressful sprint where first dates become "Is he my child's father?" interviews. She'll also start receiving well-meaning nudges from friends and aunties to get married before "those eggs dry up."

Tai considers her ten eggs on ice a gift to her future husband. "When I meet my guy and we decide to become one, get married, and start the family, we don't have to rush," she says. "I see this as only an insurance policy. I believe my perfect partner will come and we can have children naturally. I also now know I have healthy eggs if I ever need them," she says. "I think one of God's purposes for me on earth is to be a mother. That's why I have no qualms saying I took this step. God has given the great ability for scientists to conceptualize this technology, and me the means to be able to do it."

Her strategy to freeze eggs and free up the dating process is based on proven results. Lynn Marie Westphal, MD, codirector of Stanford University's Center for Health Research on Women and Sex Differences in Medicine, has performed the procedure for at least four hundred patients. "Many of the women I've seen credit freezing their eggs with helping them get into the right relationship," Dr. Westphal says. "They didn't feel like this clock was ticking and felt less stress about relationships."

Elayne and Tai both tell men they date about the frozen eggs. "It's a part of who I am and what I've done for myself," Elayne says.

Though women feel empowered and relieved after freezing their eggs, that doesn't mean everyone who has gone through the process has actually taken the final step. Many of Dr. Westphal's patients have not sought to use their frozen eggs. "Even our very first patient, who froze her eggs in the nineties, has not returned," the doctor says of the four hundred women she's seen for the procedure. "Some patients got into a relationship soon after and became pregnant naturally. Others just aren't ready to start their family yet."

For now, Tai encourages younger women to be intentional about their personal lives on her website, www.thetailife.com, and tells her peers to look into the procedure. So far, four friends are exploring the service. "Everything we want for our lives, and that we deserve, requires investment," she says. "Because I want a family, I have to invest in it. My hope is that younger women who want the same will prioritize that for themselves sooner."

Yes, facing the ticking of your biological clock can be sobering. My appointments were emotional and uncomfortable as I faced the uncertainty of fertility. I also felt empowered to learn about my body and know that I could be proactive toward achieving my pregnancy dreams. Knowing I had all the eggs I will have, including the eggs that will one day be my babies, I've started praying over my belly and also write letters to my future daughter.

No one else has the last word on our bodies and our dreams. Jill Scott learned that at an early age. "Around nineteen I went to a health clinic and was told I would not have kids and that I should have a hysterectomy," she shared at her summer concert in Newark. "Around that same age my mom went to a free clinic and they told her too to get a hysterectomy." Jill's mom did not let a diagnosis stop her from pursuing her dream of motherhood and gave birth to one of my fave singers. And Jill went on to give birth to her own son and gain five more kids through marriage.

PREGAME YOUR PREGNANCY

Don't wait until you are ready for a baby to get your body in the best position to conceive. My friend and fellow Boss Bride Latham Thomas is a renowned doula and founder of Mama Glow. She's helped some of our favorite Boss Brides become moms, including Alicia Keys and Tamera Mowry. I asked her to share tips on how to preserve your fertility. These are my favorite.

1. EAT FOR TWO. Your little one is not just made up of what you absorb during pregnancy, but what you eat now. Your body will pull nutrients from your tissues to develop your baby. Add foods to your diet that stimulate the immune system, balance hormones, and supply you with the right stuff, including whole grains, beans, nuts, vegetables, leafy greens, and fruit. Upgrade your wellness with a daily multivitamin. Your routine should include at least a 400-microgram supplement of folic acid, a B vitamin you get in green leafy veggies.

2. PROTECT YOUR OVARIES. Guard against sexually transmitted diseases. Chlamydia and gonorrhea are curable, but if left untreated can harm your reproductive system and lead to pelvic inflammatory disease (PID) and fertility issues. Up to 15 percent of women with untreated chlamydia develop PID, according to the CDC.

3. MANAGE YOUR STRESS. Did you know that stress can change the pH level and viscosity of cervical mucus, making it thicker and more challenging for you to conceive? Stress is a major obstacle to reproductive health. Using tactics like deep breathing, meditation, and physical activity are great ways to shift from stress to bliss.

4. OWN YOUR ORGASM. The uterus is a powerful player in fertility and gets a dress rehearsal for conception each time you climax. When women have a sexual release, we flood our system with endorphins that can be relaxing. An orgasm relieves the tensions on the nervous system and leads to better sleep and good moods. Embrace your primal appetite for sensual touch.

(We'll go deeper into owning your orgasm at the end of this chapter.)

Check Your Lifestyle

The hustle of being a boss isn't the same calm and loving energy of creating a new life. The BrainTrust founder Kendra Bracken-Ferguson discovered that firsthand while running a global company. "We had been trying to get pregnant for about two years in New York and then we moved to Los Angeles for a reset," she says. "I did my first ever thirty-day hot yoga challenge, religiously did acupuncture, and finally took time to breathe. While my work ethic remained just as fierce, I explored new ways of eating and living. Within two months, I was pregnant. I never would have thought my daughter would have been born in LA." When you are ready for pregnancy, review your lifestyle to be supportive of this next season.

You've Got Options

If you do want to be a mother, there are many ways that can happen. I love seeing the many ways women are making their dreams of motherhood come true from donor eggs and surrogates to adoption. There is no one right way so give yourself permission to be open to how things manifest. I loved *Today* show host Hoda Kotb's story of adopting a beautiful baby girl at age fifty-two. However love shows up, open the door.

Think Long Term

I attended the 2013 National Association of Professional Women conference. I was expecting advice on growing professionally. Instead the speakers discussed the importance of prioritizing our personal life on the quest to success with self-care and relationships. Arianna Huffington shared the story of a devastating fall due to exhaustion that made her slow down. Then Martha Stewart hit the stage.

Martha, America's first female self-made billionaire, built a lifestyle conglomerate with TV shows, books, a magazine, and merchandise that sold $1 billion a year at Kmart. The woman saw her stock prices rise when she went to jail for insider trading and came out to higher popularity with a *Fortune* cover story emblazoned with "I cannot be destroyed."

So what is the resilient entrepreneur's one regret? Does she wish she had avoided doing time? Daydreams of another career? No. Stewart shared her one regret is that she didn't have more children. Onstage she told us how she loves her daughter and wished she'd had more kids.

Get clear now on your plans for motherhood and put energy into achieving your goals.

Pregnancy and the Boss Bride

For many women, a busy career requires a major adjustment for a new baby and our work directly impacts our decisions around children. According to a 2013 New York University study of women who had frozen their eggs, 19 percent stated they would have had children earlier if their bosses were more flexible. In the book *Babygate: How to Survive Pregnancy & Parenting in the Workplace* (Feminist Press), attorneys from the work–family advocacy group A Better Balance give tips for juggling pregnancy and a career, and break down the laws that protect early motherhood.

First thing, we all have to face the sobering reality that the United States lags farther behind in honoring parenthood for new mothers and fathers than do other developed nations. As women have progressed professionally, our laws and culture have not caught up to accommodate childbirth. For low-wages positions, women worry if they will lose their job by giving birth, compared with women in the United Kingdom, which offers all women at least two weeks off from work after giving birth and up to fifty-two weeks.

WHEN AND WHAT TO SHARE

Babygate advises when to tell your manager you are expecting:

- Consider waiting until after the first trimester, the most uncertain time in a pregnancy, unless you are ill and missing a lot of work.

- Give your boss ample notice to foster goodwill and to help create a plan for while you are out.

- Review your company's leave policy and be prepared to share your wishes when you meet with your manager. Consider also meeting with HR if you have any questions.

- It is your decision to share and should be done when you are most comfortable. Don't feel pressure to disclose until you are ready, but be mindful anyone you do tell may share the news at work.

- Remember you and your baby's health come first. If you need reasonable accommodations (less travel, no heavy lifting) to protect your health, make the request to your employer.

YOUR RIGHTS

The government offers the following protections, according to *Babygate*. If you ever feel your rights are being violated, contact a lawyer.

- The Pregnancy Discrimination Act is a federal law that prohibits unfair treatment of women because of pregnancy. It was put in place because of society's pressure for pregnant women to leave the workforce. You may still be laid off or treated with hostility at work, but it can't be because of the pregnancy.

- If your employer has at least fifty employees you are covered by the Family and Medical Leave (FMLA) Act to take up to twelve weeks unpaid family leave in a year.

- What we don't have: childcare. The US Congress passed a bill to establish universal childcare in 1971 but President Nixon vetoed it.

Carrying and welcoming another life into the world is special. Pregnancy and parenting can be overwhelming. Go HARD for motherhood with Heart Actions and Researched Decisions that keep you in the driver's seat. And post any questions inside the Tribe at bossbride-tribe.com to hear from other women.

Plan Not to Have a Baby

And if you are not planning on having a baby right now, plan to not have a baby right now. Half of the pregnancies in the United States are unplanned, putting a strain on mother and baby. I have worked with Bedsider, the National Campaign's online resource to educate and empower women on contraception options and celebrate #ThxBirthControl day each November.

Many of the educational and economic opportunities women enjoy today are the result of having full access to birth control. In 1972 it became legal for single folks to use the available methods. (Before then, only married couples could.) In 2016 the National Campaign celebrated its twentieth anniversary—and a 48 percent decline in the teen pregnancy rate over the past two decades. "Deciding if, when and under what circumstances to get pregnant is arguably one of the most important life decisions a woman will make," says Ginny Ehrlich, who is the CEO of the National Campaign. "Since birth control has been made widely available, there has been a staggering increase in women's wages, an increase in female college graduates and [an improvement] in family well-being." Birth control has a definite impact on our ability to be Boss Brides. #ThxBirthControl.

There is no shame in taking charge of your future. And let's be honest: Sex is more enjoyable when you aren't stressed about a surprise pregnancy or sexually transmitted infection. A Boss Bride takes charge in every area of her life, especially the possibility of creating another life.

Now that I'm in my thirties, my mother and I have more woman-to-woman chats. In one of our conversations a few years ago, we started to talk about birth control. She let me know she got pregnant with me as soon as she took out her IUD. It was an eye-opener that more than thirty years ago she had used a birth control method I had looked into trying myself. I hadn't even thought to ask her about it.

I have many stories on the adventures of condom buying. There was the time a sales associate announced over the mic that he needed access to the locked condom shelf (yes, it's wrong that our society sells sex yet sometimes makes it so hard for people to engage responsibly). Or the time when I was visiting family down south and stocking up at Walmart, only to have my aunt come over just as the sales associate rang up four boxes.

Discussing your body and contraception is way more revealing than taking off your clothes, so talking with your partner about protecting each other from unplanned pregnancies can only increase your intimacy. It also forces both of you to actively contribute to your birth control plan since you would both be responsible for a baby. If you are comfortable enough with someone to consider getting sexually intimate, you have every right and the responsibility to ask when they've last been tested for sexually transmitted diseases and to see their results or get tested together.

Often, the most important birth control and baby planning conversation to have is with your health care provider. Make the most of your time together by already having questions in mind and not being afraid to speak up. With my gynecologist, I always bring up things I've heard from friends and family to get her perspective, since someone else's perfect method might not be a fit for me—and their problems may not apply to my individual situation.

And speaking of friends and family, they can be your own focus group on birth control. The next time you're at brunch or girls' night, bring it up. You may be surprised at what information and the variety of birth control methods and myths you discover. I found myself admiring Spike Lee's office while trying to name as many birth control options as possible. His wife and supercool Boss Bride, Tonya Lewis Lee, is a leading health advocate and was hosting a round table on birth control in their home, and we each tried to name as many birth control options as possible. I got to about eleven options.

Boss Bride Cheat Sheet to Birth Control

Here are popular options for busy women from Bedsider.org.

THE IUD A little, T-shaped piece of plastic that is put in your uterus to prevent sperm from fertilizing eggs. They offer three to twelve years of protection. Mirena, Skyla, and Liletta are hormonal. ParaGard is made of copper and nonhormonal.

THE RING NuvaRing is a small, bendable ring that you insert into your vagina for three weeks at a time, then take out for the fourth week. The ring gives off hormones that prevent your ovaries from releasing eggs.

THE SHOT Once you get it, your birth control is covered for three months. It can take between twelve weeks to nine months for fertility to return after the shot.

THE IMPLANT Nexplanon is a tiny rod (the size of a matchstick) that's inserted under the skin of your upper arm. Once effective, it prevents pregnancy for up to four years.

THE PATCH A thin, beige piece of plastic that looks like a square Band-Aid. It's a little less than two inches across and comes in only one color. You stick the patch on your skin and it gives off hormones that prevent your ovaries from releasing eggs.

THE SPONGE A round piece of white plastic foam with a little dimple on one side and a nylon loop across the top that looks like shoelace material. You insert it way up in your vagina before sex. It blocks sperm from your cervix, and it continuously releases spermicide. Think of it like a bouncer at the nightclub door to your uterus.

Owning our decisions on if and when to have children and researching our options are an essential part of owning our bodies and our sexuality.

The Ring: Your Love Below
Call your gynecologist and set up an appointment to discuss your questions and desires for fertility, contraception, and your sexual health. Your gyno is a critical player on your Love & Success Squad. Go with questions and research knowledgeable specialists in your area.

Embrace Your Sexual Self

Whether you want to have a baby or not it's your right to enjoy the experience of practicing. A few years back I hit the streets of New York with a big sign that said "Let's Talk About Sex." I walked up to women I didn't know with a camera crew and asked them: When was your last orgasm? As the granddaughter of a southern woman who avoided even saying the word "sex"—she would say "seg" if she absolutely had to reference the act—I had come a long way in finding my sexual voice as I waved women over to be interviewed for a web series. If you were born and raised on a desert island, you wouldn't miss your iPhone or know that the internet exists. But you would still have four natural desires every human is born with: for food, water, sleep, and sex.

Embrace that you were born a sexual being—even if that means setting a monthly date on your Google calendar to explore your sensuality. The more you engage with your own sexual identity, the more empowered you'll be to take charge in and outside the bedroom. There's nothing sexier than being responsible for your own destiny.

GOOD SEX FOR BOSS BRIDES

Sexologist and former *The Doctors* cohost Dr. Rachael Ross shares why physical intimacy is good for your health and how to feed your fire.

KICK YOUR CAREER OUT OF THE BED

So many of us are all about our career and it's hard to even imagine yourself letting go in the way that you need to, to really have great, dirty, raunchy sex with another person. The best sex comes when you can let yourself go, not being concerned about what your stomach looks like or whether or not you're doing the right thing and just be in the moment. Sometimes a woman's mind wanders and they're thinking about a lot of the wrong things. Block everything else out. That hardworking executive woman who barely has time to date, if she would take five or ten minutes at the end of her day and just focus on connecting with her own sexual energy, that type of energy will exude from her and she'll start to become a sexier person.

STAY SEXUALLY ALIVE

I have one patient who is forty-five and hasn't had sex in ten years. When you're taking a long break your clitoris and your vagina go to sleep. It's a muscle. If you don't use it, you will lose it and that connection to yourself. It can take a lot of effort to try to re-create that. If a woman has gone three years without any sexual activity with herself or someone else, she is at that threshold. I find that people who give up on intimacy, who don't really have anybody that they're being close to, connected to, hugging, kissing, or holding hands with, you actually see an increase in cortisol, your stress level. It's a very comforting relief when you have intimate relations with someone else and that's not just sex. Outercourse is grinding, massaging, kissing, fondling, and bringing someone to orgasm without pene-tration.

PREGAME YOUR PLEASURE

The first thing that a woman has to do is recognize that your sex drive starts in your brain. So, if you're stressed out, over-worked, or only thinking about your job, it's really hard for sex to creep its way in there. Our sex drive as women doesn't start in the car like it does for a guy, or when we're doing dishes. Our sex drive often starts with an initiation of sex. Your initiation of sex can be with sexual thoughts or sexual visual aids or audio aids. It's flirting with someone in per-son or through text messages, reading an erotic book or watching a movie that turns you on. To really know what pleasure is and what feels good to you and where your spot really is for yourself. My first orgasm, like a lot of women will tell you, was by myself.

KEEP YOUR SPARK

The couple that really continues to have strong sex drives are the ones who are always doing something different. It helps keep the brain constantly stimulated in new and exciting ways. It's important that you not do the same thing every time or else it gets boring and dull.

- Find safe, public places to have sexual encounters.

- Sext for the day and then plan a quickie.

- Make sure that there's a little moisture down there before he arrives by stimulating yourself a little bit or dab a little lubrication down. We feel like a man is attracted to us and wants it if he has an erection. For men, they feel like we really want it and we're really attracted to them if we're moist.

- Remember your guy's testicles and his nipples are a part of his sexual repertoire and very sensitive areas. Guys are really connected to you if you remember that they're there. And don't save a blow job for special occasions. There is power in it.

One of the best gifts you can give yourself is to fully tap into your sensuality. Sexuality can be one of our most powerful energy sources, so it's important for women to tap into our sexual selves on our own terms. A satisfying sex life boosts our health and well-being.

Like every area of life, sometimes our sex lives can become routine. It's important to continue trying new experiences to keep the excitement and refresh your libido. Whether it's making the first move or letting your alter ego out at dinner, bring your fantasies to life.

Angel, a popular oral sex expert from Chicago, was married with little experience performing oral sex when she decided she wanted to upgrade her skills on going down. She began to experiment and soon started sharing what she learned with friends. "Oral sex is about pleasure for both of us," she shares. Now she creates popular DVD tutorials and has taught classes for more than forty-five thousand women. When she was in New York I had her stop by the office and meet with our editors. Of course hosting a fellatio how-to raised a few eyebrows, but it was worth it for women to feel as confident in the bedroom as we do in the boardroom.

THE BOSS BRIDE CHEAT SHEET: TURN UP YOUR SEXY

- Invest in luxurious new lingerie and sleepwear

- Sign up for burlesque classes

- Look in the mirror naked every day for a week and find something new to compliment each time

- Book a boudoir photo shoot

- Fall asleep on a cloud with a comforting mattress, pillows, and sheets and enjoy your new bedding in the nude

- Find a new sultry scent

- Add muted lighting to your bedroom to set the mood

Save the Date:
Embrace Your Sexuality and Femininity

Commit to trying something exciting and fresh from the cheat sheet or something you've always wanted to explore in the next month. Feeding your innate sexuality is a gift to your soul.

Push to do whatever it takes to feel like a goddess. The more turned-on you are by your own self, the more unstoppable you become. Many parts of this book were written in my furry pale pink kitten heels I snagged in Paris a few years back. They remind me of the sensual woman I get to be. I was sure to bring them along when I did my first boudoir photo shoot with photographer and Boss Bride Ilene Squires. I'm also a trained burlesque dancer after signing up for the Broad Squad Institute and a regular in Zumba and belly dancing classes.

My Burlesque Debut

"Breathe into your p*ssy," said Chicava HoneyChild, producer and proprietor of Brown Girls Burlesque. Ten women of varying shades and shapes sat in butterfly position inside a New York City dance studio wondering what we'd got ourselves into. We were the newest recruits of the Broad Squad Institute, a six-week intro course to burlesque, the legendary dance form that mixes storytelling and striptease. The physical stretching had nothing on the class's psychological push to unleash our sensual selves. "Decide what part of your body or life you want to reclaim with burlesque," Chicava encouraged. "Explore your fantasies, desires, and the things that bother you." In these days of butt shots, slut walks, and backside selfies, women need the space to define and celebrate our bodies and sexuality more than ever.

I got that opportunity as each of us in the class popped out a nipple and tried on pasties of different sizes to cover our areolae. I chose purple pasties and champagne tassels as my first burlesque accessory: I was officially a dancer. Next the bras came off—we taped on our pasties and the fun began as we tried to get the tassels to twirl. I soon discovered I have a breast twin. With clothes on, we could be cousins. But with bras off, we could be sisters. I laughed and bounced. The free-flowing feminine energy was exhilarating, and the experience was one of the most intimate of my life. Next we put the tassels on our pants or undies and tried to twirl the tassels with our butts. This isn't about turning someone else on but about reveling in our beauty and our bodies.

Every burlesque dancer needs a moniker. For our second class, a few graduates of the institute came and shared the backstory of their burlesque names, including sassaBrass: The Poom Poom Priestess. "I'm a pleasure filled healer who uses performance to deliver the gospel of the p*ssy," she shares on her website. "Welcome to a church where we p*ssy-pop for praise, twerk for testimony and worship in service of our liberation." I'm in love with her fusion of spirituality and sex, something I've been fighting to unite as a sexual being and granddaughter of a southern minister. My mother, like her mother, skipped the sex talk with her daughter. I'm determined to end the silence on sexuality that plagued my family and many others. The next morning in the shower, words that feel southern and feminine sashayed around in my mind. Peaches. Molasses. Sweet potato. Finally my burlesque name came to me: Soufflé. The dish that makes everyday sweet potatoes sound chic fits me like a nipple tassel.

In the week we learned how to seductively take off stockings and gloves, a friend excitedly shared that she was getting fat taken out of her stomach and put into her butt. I invited her to check out the class. My butt didn't get bigger from going, but I did fall deeper in love with the body I'm blessed with. "Plastic surgery won't cure self-esteem issues," Chicava says. "We all have things we want to change. The first step is to accept yourself. Then to celebrate that you are a complete, unique phenomenon."

I remembered her words during my first burlesque performance to a mash-up of Ray Charles's "Georgia on My Mind" and Beyoncé and Nicki Minaj's "Feeling Myself." I own my body, one shake at a time.

Whispers of a Woman
WHAT EACH WORKING WIFE WOULD SAY TO HERSELF AS SHE WALKED DOWN THE AISLE

Love as well as "like" each other. **Don't get bogged down with the small stuff.** Remember there is no perfect person and know that everyday will not always be sunshine. Juggling marriage and a career will not be easy and remember that you are marrying someone who knows your worth and will support you. **Let it be.** Take in this special moment and fully enjoy it because reality comes quick after the honeymoon. We all think that our husbands are our knight in shining armor but reality is that we both are works in progress and when you return to work leave home business at home. The famous question that will be asked is "how was it"; that's personal and I do not wish to share my personal business. **Always remember, you are BEST friends.** Learn how to manage and juggle the time so God is first, husband second, and job last. **Everything you need is contained in this man. Just trust God.** I found my pot of gold.

Be careful what you wish for . . . you just might get it.

8

UNLEASH HAPPILY
EVER NOW

The biggest adventure you can take is to live the life of your dreams.
—OPRAH WINFREY

It's finally my big day, not something I've planned for someone else. I feel like royalty after Atlanta stylist Michael Gillespie escorted me to Ivy Showroom in Buckhead to find the perfect dress and Cynthia Bailey personally picked a pair of shades from her eyewear collection for me. I feel sleek and photo-ready in the textured frock and ready for my entrance.

And where am I going? Well, to The Promised Land: Oprah's 65-acre estate in California. Instead of a book tour to launch *Wisdom of Sundays: Life-Changing Insights from Super Soul Conversations*, she has decided to host a private gospel brunch on her lawn. While in Atlanta for another event, I got invited to join an intimate round table interview with Oprah and a few journalists in her garden before the event begins. Like I shared in Chapter 1, I missed my first chance to meet the motivational mogul and was determined to meet her and did. So this unexpected invite on a Sunday I happen to be in LA? Well, we will get to that in a minute.

But first you want to know what the experience was like and I want to tell you.

The first thing you notice upon entering Oprah Winfrey's estate are the trees. She previously shared that early in her career she visited a mentor's house and noticed the trees in her yard. Oprah surmised that rich people own trees and, one day, she would own six herself. Her Montecito, CA, estate has more than 3,600 trees. I checked in close by and was escorted with some other reporters by golf cart through a winding driveway woven through gorgeous green grass and trees. We passed by a huge fountain where in the distance you could see the main home and a pond that had candles all around it. We parked near her guest home and walked along a lush walkway to get to the garden.

Soon entered the reigning queen of media and philanthropy. She sat with us and talked about her commitment to continuing to help awaken others. "That's such a wonderful question," she said, staring deeply into my eyes, after I asked how she had adjusted to a life bigger than anything she had imagined, making a leap from growing up in rural Mississippi to this estate in Montecito, and the magical journey in between. Her answer? Never missing the beauty of the present moment. "There's not a day that I wake up here, that I don't have a sense of appreciation and gratitude. Usually on Sunday mornings, I'm around with the dogs. There's not a day I don't walk the property and find something different. I find another piece of moss growing between stones, or I'll turn my head and I'll look back through a tree and I've never looked through that tree, at that angle, before." That commitment to witnessing your life is why I first created my course Happily Ever Now, to share with others the magic in loving our lives, which led me to that table. After gliding into the garden, it was time for the main event. But first Oprah stood to take pictures with each of us. Before my photo I had to tell her about Charanna and Jimmy, my good friends who were getting married that day and the reason I was even in Los Angeles. She recorded a beautiful wedding blessing for them, and then noticed my stiletto sandals. I had not gotten the memo not to wear heels. "You want some flats?" she asked. Who says "no" to Lady

O? "I'll bring you rose gold," she said, noting the shoes I was wearing. We used the restroom in her guest home. I was wowed looking at the bookcase and her desk, which housed a photo of her and Nelson Mandela and one with her and Maya Angelou.

We walked to the outside amphitheater. Oprah walked by with a bag holding flats after heading inside her closet to grab shoes for me and another woman in heels. I was stunned by her personal care and looked at the metallic Lanvin. They were a little too big on me, but who really expects to fit Oprah's shoes? I found a seat in the outside theater housing 200 of her friends and Super Soul leaders. She soon took the stage. "It's not often I open this space. Stedman and I welcome you to what we call The Promised Land. I use to call it Tara II," she shared. "One day I was looking out the back lawn to the ocean and said, 'Scarlett O'Hara wishes she lived here.' I get to live the promise Dr. King had for all of us. I welcome you here to The Promised Land."

And welcomed I felt. I realized the couple sitting in front of me were *Star Wars* creator George Lucas and my ultimate Boss Bride crush and business leader Mellody Hobson. Julia Roberts sat with her husband, Danny Moder, near Oprah and Stedman Graham. Diane Von Furstenberg sat next to Diane Sawyer with Shonda Rhimes nearby and Arianna Huffington holding down the aisle seat. Kerry Washington and Angela Bassett were up rocking and clapping along with the choir. The concert was led by Bebe Winans, who took the choir and crowd through a medley of classic gospel songs. Yolanda Adams, Erica Campbell, and Andra Day blessed the mic as Common also joined Day to perform their new song "Stand Up for Something." Cynthia Erivo closed out the show. Guests then walked to an open lawn reminiscent of Eden for Sunday brunch produced by Colin Cowie. I walked around to take in the brunch and powerful crowd. "Charreah," I heard as Niecy Nash, attending with her mom, called me over. And when Mindy Kaling and her adorable baby bump walked over to say "hi" to Niecy she graciously introduced me. And then it was time to go.

I understood how Cinderella felt with the clock ticking over my head at the most magical event of my life. Instead of turning into a pumpkin, my fear was being late to my friend's wedding when I was a bridesmaid! I made it back in time to slip into my gorgeous gold dress that I really would wear again if it wasn't rented from Vow To Be Chic.

Tick. Tock. Tick. Tock. Tickkk. Tockkkkk.

The future just passed you by. Every second you've spent reading this book (and I salute you for making it to the final chapter) was once the future. And now it is the past.

Once you find and own your Boss Bride, it's important that you honor her every day and that you soak in all of life's magic every chance you get. The most fulfilled women keep their feet planted in the present and are always willing to make this day their best yet. Being a Boss Bride is not a destination or item to check off your to-do list. Your joy and fulfillment is a daily habit. What makes you smile deserves to be a priority.

Create Your Crazy 8

As life kicks up, keep giving yourself permission to dream big and try again. So often we limit our desires, thinking things or people are outside our reach. In reality there are a million ways your dream can come true. Once I owned I wanted to meet Oprah all the ways it could happen started to flood my mind. I have a practice called the Crazy 8 for big goals where I list eight ways my dream could come true. Want to send ten girls to school or take a selfie with the Rock? Think of eight ways it could happen. You will be surprised the options you unlock when you use your imagination to design our own life.

You Are Bigger Than Your Biggest Fear

I wanted to see more women get off the sidelines of our own lives and run toward our joy, so I launched Happily Ever Now, a six-week online course to help women fall in love with their lives.

Of course the fear of launching my own course was heavy with all the things that could go wrong. And I did it anyway as Module 5 breaks down how to grab hold of fear. I had confronted fear the summer before with a mouthful of salt water. I was out on a beach on Far Rockaway in New York for my first surfing lesson. After learning the basics of surfing it was time for us to get in the water and try to catch a wave. We paddled out into the water and then turned around facing the shore to get ready to ride a wave. The instructors would yell "Pop up" when it was the right moment to try to stand up on the board and surf. It was scary as the waves kept coming. The first time I tried to pop up my feet slipped and I was quickly underwater. The second time I moved too slowly and the wave got me down. The third time I popped up and rode my first wave.

I was officially a surfer and there wasn't much you could say to me. Walking on the shore after riding a wave, I looked back at the water and saw other women on the trip deep in the water with dry hair. They would put their knees on the board and ride the waves, but never try to stand. They weren't willing to risk falling underwater, and were also not willing to reach for their chance to stand up and surf, an incredible high.

I could see how fear robs us of the opportunities we are meant to have. Our greatest joys come with real risks. The secret is to know we are bigger than our biggest fears. We can always get back up, even when the wind is knocked out of us.

I launched my Happily Ever Now course on January 2, 2017, my first two days of the year full of my frazzled nerves and malfunctions in the midst of Mercury in her retroshade. I was fighting tears and internet glitches when Facebook Memories showed me my happy New Year post from 2016. On it was a comment from Daisy Lewellyn.

The world knew Daisy as an over-the-top star on Bravo's *Blood, Sweat & Heels*. I knew her as a kindred spirit, friend, and fellow Howard grad and magazine editor. She worked on the fashion team at *Essence* when I started as an assistant shortly after graduation. And our love of print dresses and, well, being loud, bonded us. We also went to the same church, FCBC in Harlem, where she created DREAMNYC, a program for high school students to learn about media. I hosted the group at my office. We talked books and men, as she launched her book *Never Pay Retail* with a chic cocktail party at Tracy Reese's flagship boutique in Soho and a digital rerelease on the show at a swanky Thai restaurant. I supported her at both.

And when I wrote about my cancer journey in *Essence*, she called me to talk about her own diagnosis that would soon be announced on the show. Months after entering 2016 and writing that comment, Daisy was gone after her cancer had returned.

Seeing her message as I started a new year she never got to see stopped me with sadness. It also compelled me to be urgent with the message of Happily Ever Now.

Every breath we take and day we enter is a gift. We honor being alive by fully living. If there was any comfort in Daisy dying at thirty-six, it was the reality she had not wasted any of her short time. She had gone full out for the life she wanted, including moving across the country multiple times, launching TV projects, and helping other young women on their journey. We each get to go full out for the life we desire and be urgent with our dreams.

On my list of women I would have loved to interview for this book sits Amy Krouse Rosenthal. She was an acclaimed writer and went viral in early 2017 with her *New York Times* Modern Love essay, "You May Want to Marry My Husband." In it she shares her twenty-six-year love story with Jason as she battles ovarian cancer and writes a pseudo dating profile for the love of her life and father of her kids. Even though I never met Amy, her life touched mine. In her 2010 TED Talk she shows the magic of a try after inviting anyone interested to a day of making things together. Hundreds show up and the video is pure magic. Yes, you should watch. And though I'm sure Amy would have loved more time on the planet, she squeezed joy and sunshine out of her time.

Your happiness and joy are not for later. They are on today's menu. As much as I would love to tell you your dream life will be sitting in a box when you get home tonight, it's not. And you already knew that. That still doesn't stop us from sometimes daydreaming about our own fairy tales to finally begin. We sometimes hold on to hope that we will be saved from ourselves.

As Alice Walker said more than twenty years ago and President Obama brought back in 2009, we are the ones we have been waiting for.

The cavalry is not coming to bring us our dream lives. No one is at home thinking what a great catch you are and checking Facebook to see which of their fabulous friends should take you out. Our partners aren't daydreaming of ways to surprise us at work tomorrow with a sexy weekend getaway (well, not until you train him to do so).

And that's the good news. The bad news is when we don't realize the power we have to be whoever the hell we want and live the lives we hope for.

You Have the Right to Change Your Mind

One of the most powerful freedoms in the Boss Bride Bill of Rights is the right to change your mind. Your time is too precious to continue to do things that no longer serve you.

At any moment you can say NO to something you've been wanting your whole life and say YES to something or someone you have actively avoided.

I sat courtside at a New York Knicks game because best-selling author and health advocate J. J. Smith changed her mind. Years before she went on a job interview that lasted for hours. She realized she had chemistry with Todd, who was interviewing her. "You can either have the job or we can go on a date," he offered. She chose the date. "I can get another job," she said with a laugh. The two dated then married. Then realized they were better as friends than spouses. And now he is her business partner helping her run a global healthy living empire. And they invited me to join them at the game. We had a blast (read: talking sh*t and the players can hear you) and I was reminded we can always shift our circumstances to what works for us NOW.

One of the most iconic Boss Brides is Gloria Steinem, the legendary feminist and vocal critic of marriage for thirty years. So many of the freedoms we enjoy as women and Boss Brides is because of the work of Steinem and feminists around the globe.

In 2000, Steinem said YES to being an actual bride for the first time, at sixty-six. She wed entrepreneur David Bale, sixty-one, in a small ceremony in rural Oklahoma.

"Though I've worked many years to make marriage more equal, I never expected to take advantage of it myself. I'm happy, surprised and one day will write about it, but for now, I hope this proves what feminists have always said—that feminism is about the ability to choose what's right at each time of our lives," she shared in a statement from Voters for Choice, a political action committee she helped start.

Getting married was big news for Steinem, who tirelessly fought for the equality of women and had previously said "a woman needs a man like a fish needs a bicycle."

Steinem and her new husband gave their first interview as newlyweds to Barbara Walters for ABC. Here are snippets of this juicy interview.

GLORIA STEINEM ON GETTING MARRIED

If the marriage law was the same law that it was before the women's movement thirty years ago. I wouldn't have been able to do it. I would have lost most of my civil rights. I would have lost my name, my credit rating, my legal domicile, the ability to start a business. Really most civil rights. And also, I was a happy single person for fifty years. This is a long time.

ON HER HUSBAND

He's, um, an adventurer, and intelligent, and funny, and compassionate, and a pilot. You might look at him and think this is, you know, a macho person or something. And he's a person who has also raised his own children. That plus many things in his life have made him somebody who totally defies the idea that men are from Mars and women are from

Venus and who really proves that we're all from Earth. We love each other and this is the most important thing that we really want to be together, that we were together every minute for a month, which neither of us had ever done before and loved it. Why make it legal? Because we both felt that we wanted to be responsible for each other.

Sadly, soon after they married David Bale was diagnosed with brain lymphoma and he passed in 2003. He was able to get medical treatment on Steinem's insurance since they were legally married. "It was terrible, terrible, the two years of his illness and afterwards. But, looking back, there was a purpose," she said to *The Guardian*. "His purpose in my life was to make me feel deeply, and to live in the present. Because I live in the future. My purpose was to give him something that he hadn't had. We discovered that he liked to travel with me, and after an event, he would have five hundred young women around him, all so relieved to see that you can be a feminist and have a relationship with a man—and he was so excited by it. At Smith [College], he would walk around campus saying: 'Which one of these young women is going to be president?' And then . . . I ushered him out of life. His kids were there, and they were wonderful, but a contemporary is a different thing. In a way, he taught me about dying."

Gloria Steinem went six decades rallying against the institution of marriage only to fall in love, get married, and lose her husband less than three years later. And she doesn't regret any of it.

"It is better to have loved and lost than to never have loved at all." I first heard these words in high school while watching the film *Ever After*, where Drew Barrymore stars as a can-do Cinderella. She holds her own, stands up for the less fortunate, and ends up falling for the prince. Very Boss Bride.

When I heard that quote I was skeptical. Was it really better to have loved and lost? Would it be better to wish for something you've never had than to endure the pain of losing it?

As Gloria Steinem and my parents' wedding album show, the answer is yes. Love is absolutely worth it. And when you've really been loved, nothing can ever take away the sweetness of those memories and the broadness of your heart.

Embrace Your Evolution

Our past is not only fuel for our next chapters, but can also be the catalyst for us to get there. As you build the courage to grow and shed expired seasons, toxic relationships, and past pain, it can be tempting to want to hide where you've come from. "So beautiful. What happened?" my aunt asked a few weeks after my breakup. I told her it was good for a while but I wanted more than that relationship offered. My aunt had been my muse, a stunning chemist who never fully recovered from her divorce. I spent my life weary yet wanting love, determined not to let heartbreak grab the best of me. We sat at my grandparents' house a few feet from the front porch where my parents wed more than thirty years before. Later that night I flipped through my parents' wedding photos. I looked at the young smiling faces, grateful that they found each other even if it wasn't meant to be forever. Their demise was my reality check that relationships aren't fairy tales and require work. My parents' divorce not only shaped my life, but my career. The Friday after my split I was on a plane home to Atlanta to receive an editor of the year award from the AAMBC Literary Awards. While in town my mom and I got a couple's massage side-by-side at a spa downtown. I finally opened up on the things that weren't working in the relationship that I'd hidden from her and so many, not wanting to paint my former partner in a bad light. Owning how I got to my current spot gave me freedom to start dreaming again. I knew I was stronger than my biggest fear—heartbreak— and I was strong enough to love again. I wrote my list of what I desired and a few months later Sir Brooklyn showed up at my table.

Every day you get to pick up the pen and write your own story. A friend who has the stunning house, gorgeous family, banging body, and designer wardrobe recently opened up on the reality that before she and her husband married, he'd had a one-night stand that ended with a set of twins around her son's age. What could have broken many couples became the ground they rebuilt their relationship on. "Had I listened to what others said, I would have left," she says. "I'm so glad I stayed and we haven't looked back."

The Ring: Say Thank You

"It doesn't have to be lonely at the top—take people with you." I love this quote by Mikki Taylor, which speaks to the importance of our Love & Success Squad as we grow. For your final connection challenge, reach out to three people who have been instrumental in your journey and love story—and simply say "Thank you." The more gratitude we feel, the more we have room to receive.

The Sun Is Always Shining

One of the perks of traveling a lot is that I get to hang out in the sky (I'm currently on a plane to St. Louis after being in South Africa last week and heading to Atlanta tomorrow). And one of the things I love most is to fly when it's overcast. On a cloudy day we take off with no sun in sight and gloomy weather. And as the plane ascends into the sky there she is, shining bright. I try to remember that on the rough days in my life, the sun shines every single day, even when we can't see it. To be a Boss Bride is to embrace the lows that come with life's highs. To remember on the cloudy days that the sun is still out. In the midst of writing this book one of my dearest friends lost her dad unexpectedly. It was a few months after my first boss lost her husband, the father of her two young kids, in a car accident. The tragedies rocked me as I grieved for two people I love. Committing to be your best self does not come with a guarantee everything will happen the way you want. Knowing that nothing is promised is our permission slip to go full out for what we do want. To find the goodness in the good days knowing that tomorrow will have its own set of circumstances. To relish when the sun comes out. Life is the present moment and love is our secret weapon. Our strength is in not needing for it all to be together to still stand tall and choose to love.

In 2011 community leader and entrepreneur Resurrection Graves found herself at a homeless shelter. Resurrection had leased a two-thousand-square-foot building for her massage business, lived in a three-thousand-square-foot home, and was in a bad relationship. In a few months' time she'd closed the business, lost her home, and ended the relationship. She was living in her car when Hurricane Irene and an earthquake hit Washington, DC. She whispered a special prayer. "I asked God to make clear what would end this cycle," Resurrection shares. "His instructions were clear. He told me to go to a particular homeless shelter in Virginia, and I did." It was there she felt the stare of a man from across the room. One night she was sitting outside of the shelter on a covered porch watching the rain. Deven came over and introduced himself. She learned he was an army veteran working to get back on his feet. Their connection was instant though Graves was hesitant after all she had experienced. Deven was consistent in his care for her, even with limited resources, including walking five miles to Resurrection's job at a local grocery store just to bring her lunch, then making the return trek.

However, a fairy-tale ending was hard to imagine as the two both fought to get their lives stable again. "I told myself that I refused to fall completely until I could see that he could overcome homelessness and work a reliable job," she says. Soon after, a business acquaintance that had no idea that Resurrection was homeless reached out to her. He shared a business opportunity for veterans in the DC area. "I felt this was the final sign I needed," she says. "Deven worked full-time and it transformed our life. He proved himself to be faithful, diligent, and a provider with integrity." As the couple started to make plans for their future and marriage, Deven received a housing opportunity that could only include Graves and her daughter if they were married. "He told me, 'I don't want to live without you. I want you with me,'" she recalls. "I was in total shock that 'the one' had finally come. And, I felt this overwhelming sense of gratefulness to God."

Resurrection had attended the unveiling of the Martin Luther King, Jr. Memorial on August 28, 2011. Afterward she had returned to the shelter and Deven struck up a conversation with her. "After this conversation on the 28th, we've never stopped talking." Two years later, the couple decided to marry at the Jefferson Memorial on August 28, 2013, the fiftieth anniversary of the historic March on Washington and Dr. King's "I Have a Dream" speech. "Romans 8:28 is also very fitting to our life, our relationship, and what God has done for us," Resurrection says.

The couple marched to the monument to pledge their lives together, and were joined by their minister and loved ones. Once again rain fell from the sky. "I've always seen rain as a sign of cleansing and harvest," Resurrection shares.

While most couples obsess over wedding cakes and DJs, these newlyweds had something else in mind for their reception. After marrying on the National Mall, they fulfilled another of Dr. King's messages: feeding the hungry. The duo and their guests visited several parks around Washington, DC, and offered food to homeless men and women. The husband and wife are cofounders of Glory Soldiers Global, an organization to help end poverty and homelessness. "After I got into the shelter and met Deven, there were many confirmations that he was indeed the reason that I ended up there," she says.

I first wrote about Resurrection's story in *Essence* after she emailed me to share her journey and it has always been one of my favorites. Years later, she and Deven are still going strong and helping others in need. When single women ask where to meet men I remind them love can show up where you least expect it—even at a homeless shelter. When we let go of how things should turn out we create space to be wowed. Trust that things are always working out for your good even when it doesn't look like it. The sun is always shining.

Manage Your Journey

There are a lot of things you can't control—and there is even more in life that you absolutely can be proactive about. To keep your relationship with yourself and your partner strong through life's highs and lows requires consistent care and attention. To do that requires keeping inventory of what's working and what's not.

Part of Going HARD and going home is to implement regular check-ins. In January and July I do check-ins to review my goals for the year and how I am doing emotionally, physically, financially, and in my relationships. I review my diary entries, calendar, and get present to what's working and what's not. The happiest couples I know do the same together. Add a calendar invite for January and June to take inventory of your life and witness where you have been.

Working Wife Confession: Goal Model

Actress Holly Robinson Peete and Rodney Peete's solid twenty-year marriage in Hollywood with four children isn't magic. It's evidence of what's possible when you implement a strategy for a strong partnership. Here are some of their top tips from our *Essence* interview.

1. **Get professional support.** "From the beginning Rodney was willing to sit down with a counselor," Holly says. "Most brothers I know and that I dated would never do that. We sat down with an objective third party. That was crucial in the early days of our relationship, with our busy schedules. We still have our counselor in our lives." Rodney also credits those sessions with helping start their marriage strong: "We laid it all out on what we expected and what the guidelines were. And we followed it."

2. **Befriend strong couples.** For their twentieth anniversary Rodney surprised Holly with a couples' night out to celebrate. They were joined by their tribe of strong couples. "I can get on the phone with any of our friends' circle and not feel like I'm gossiping about my husband. Some-

times you just need to vent," Holly says. "We've tried to build a community of people that have integrity. We are not perfect but we are supported."

3. **Work as a team.** The number of women leaning on men for financial security is shrinking, and the Peetes are proud to be a part of that progression. "What made me most comfortable with Rodney was that he was not threatened by the fact that I had my own life and money," Holly recalls. Decades later, the Peetes still shake off traditional gender roles: "Society tells us you're less of a man if your wife is more successful. I don't buy into any of that," Rodney says. "If I've got to take the kids to practice or a concert because she's on the road filming, I have no problem with that, because it's a partnership and a family."

What's Working for the Working Wives

Keeping love at the top of your to-do list leads to consistent joy. Here are the habits for happiness.

"Creating vision boards together, taking time out for us, giving him my undivided attention, listening to his words, but more importantly his feelings."

"We do a marriage check-in, where we ask what grade we would give our marriage. We share any positives and negatives. We keep the triangle, God at the top, then he and I on each corner."

"Keeping myself interesting and being the girlfriend having hot sex. Taking time for fun getaways. Asking outright how are you feeling about us."

"Knowing the expectations of your spouse. Whether it's spending a certain amount of quality time together or who's responsible for washing the dishes."

"My husband and I commit to taking a trip once a quarter. If you find date night to be difficult once a week, try to add a date luncheon, date morning, or date brunch to your calendar. That works for us. Also, we love daytime movie dates. We have the theater to ourselves. Plus, the price is super-low. I find daytime dating of my husband to be so romantic and intimate."

"Be honest, even when it hurts or makes you look and feel bad."

"What keeps us strong is deciding what is best for us and blocking out everyone else. We take other opinions into consideration, but once we decide how we're going to spend our money, what we will and won't tolerate in our house, who we spend our time with, it's settled."

"We pray! We have check-ins with a seasoned married couple who did our premarital counseling. We make it a priority to get away at least once every two months."

"No one will ever see me argue with him. That doesn't mean we don't argue but I'm not belittling him for anyone to see."

"Support each other and make our home a refuge from the stresses of careers."

Throughout the process of writing this to you I've constantly been taking my own advice. After dating Sir Brooklyn for a few months we realized we both still had healing to do from our previous relationships and transitioned to friends. I realized I was so used to being in a relationship I needed a little more time to be single with Charreah. That's when I took a deeper examination of my dating habits and expanded my single sea. I grabbed more of my power and committed to getting ready for my future marriage. Unexpectedly I reconnected with one of the first single men I had profiled for *Essence*. He was the only guy I've interviewed that I could see myself dating. He was still single and even more captivating. We'll call him Ken because he's straight out of a fairy tale with gorgeous looks, strong values, and running a successful company with confidence and style. Will I end up with Sir Brooklyn, Ken, or some incredible person I have yet to meet? I don't know but you can ask me about it when we meet. What I do know is the man I marry is one lucky guy, as my own love story has already begun. I've made vows to myself that make everything I touch covered in glitter.

Welcome to your happily ever now. As a Boss Bride, you are a butterfly—courageous enough to shed your old self, discover your beauty, and fly. Keep picking up the pen and writing your own next chapter.

Whispers of a Woman
WHAT EACH WORKING WIFE WOULD SAY TO HERSELF AS SHE WALKED DOWN THE AISLE

Run, girl, run! I'm kidding. I would whisper you did good with this one, he will support your dreams, push you to be better and always remind you how amazing you are even when your clients make you feel unworthy. Be open and honest about everything. **DO YOU!** Keep it real and continue to do the things that brought us together. **Spend more time and money on travel.** Look at the big picture when going through difficult times. **New life requires a different way of organizing things.** Love up-flows. Be willing to work at it even when it's hard. **Don't let perfect be the enemy of good.** It's not going to be easy but it's worth it. **Don't do anything because you feel like you are supposed to. Learn to live and thrive on your own before becoming a couple with someone.** Pray and trust God's plan. **Breathe. You know your priorities.** Let the little stuff go. **Marry someone you like and who makes you laugh. It will make the tough days shorter. Do your best and know it is enough. P.S. Don't forget to take care of you too.** Don't take people or life so seriously. It's all temporary.

I'd love to stay connected. If you've downloaded your free playbook (and I know you did) at www.bossbride.com/playbook then stay tuned for an email from me to help you get the most out of the info in this book.

ACKNOWLEDGMENTS

Thank you first to YOU the Boss Bride who just finished reading this book. Your commitment to yourself makes the world better. Please be sure to complete your playbook and do leave a review on Amazon to let me know what you thought of the book.

This book was a labor of love. Emphasis on "labor" and even more love.

It was the love of my girl Adenike Olanrewaju, who sent my book proposal to agent Regina Brooks, founder of Serendipity Literary Agency. That proposal was three ideas and seven years ago. Thank you, Regina, for seeing something in me and signing me as a client. It took us four years for the right idea to develop and for me to grow into the woman to write it. I am grateful your patience rubbed off.

Thank you to my editor, Monique Patterson, at St. Martin's Press. You got it from the beginning and trusted me so much it made me nervous. Your standing in your power gave me a chance to stand in mine.

To Cynthia Hutto Jackson, the Boss Bride that birthed me literally, spiritually, and emotionally, thank you for your unwavering love, and fostering my love of books and leading the way to womanhood. To Myrtha, Naomi, Katie, and Cora, my grandmothers and their mothers: your shoulders I stand on and your stories I carry.

To the Boss Bride Tribe that motivated me to keep going, thank you. Your passion and vision stun me. Renelda, you are the MVBB. (Join us at bossbridetribe.com.)

To my *Essence* crew, I got my master's in womanhood serving with you. It is a sorority I am forever grateful to have entered. It has been an honor to work alongside some of the world's most brilliant minds and evolve with this legendary media company.

To the women writers and editors who paved the way, I salute you. The ones that personally mentored me: Yanick Rice Lamb, Joyce Davis, Wendy Wilson, Sharon Boone Wright, Marcia Gillespie, Mitzi Miller, Demetria Lucas, Marie Brown, Jacklyn Monk, and Denene Millner. And the ones who spoke to me from the page: Lorraine Hansberry, Audre Lorde, Zora Neale Hurston, and Pearl Cleage.

To my friends and fellow authors Luvvie Ajayi, Joi-Marie Mckenzie, and Sheri Riley, who helped me feel normal in this intense season, thank you for checking on me and letting me follow in your footsteps.

To the Working Wives in my life who proved for me you don't have to choose between great love and toe-curling success, and whispered in my ear along the way, thank you: Tami Wells Thomas, Earline Barnes, Tanisha Sykes, Nicole Roberts Jones, Patrice Washington, Marsha Haygood, Mikki Taylor, Yvette Noel-Schure, and many more.

To my personal tribe: Celeste Young, Charanna Alexander, Kelly Davis, Michael Arceneaux, Katie-Marie Fickling, Tia Canty Wright, Arion Jamerson, Shani Barnes Maymon, and Aisha Barnes. I don't make it easy to hang with me. You don't let that stop you. Thanks for loving me while I was still finding who that was.

To the O'Berry, Hutto, Jackson, and Howard families, I am thankful your blood runs through my veins. Thank you for being my soft place in the world since birth. We are blessed with a spiritual inheritance money can't buy.

To my siblings and soul tribe: Deja, Jermaine, and Tina.

To my spiritual sisters who guided me: Zya (Zya.global), Charmaine Alexander, and Latham Thomas.

To my Momentum Education family, thank you for lifting this loving, trusting, and connected woman. It is because of the stand of Robin Lynn and my mentor Sylvia High that this book exists. To my coaches Lisa Nichols and Jullien Gordon, who have guided me on the journey, thank you for seeing me.

To the men I've loved and who have loved me, thank you.

To my coauthor, thank you. I did not have a ghostwriter, but I did have a God writer. God was present every step of the way for this project. On the early mornings I didn't want to get out of bed, on the days I didn't have it, I would feel God's presence and spirit working through me and the pages filled with what you were meant to read. I thank God for trusting me to write this, when there were many times I felt far from being a Boss or a Bride. God loves you and guided our paths to cross with this book. My prayer is that it blesses you as you bless the world.